ACLS History E-Book Project
Reprint Series

The ACLS History E-Book Project (www.historyebook.org) collaborates with constituent societies of the American Council of Learned Societies, publishers, librarians and historians to create an electronic collection of works of high quality in the field of history. This volume is produced from digital images created for the Project by the Scholarly Publishing Office and the Digital Library Production Service at the University of Michigan, Ann Arbor. The digital reformatting process results in an electronic version of the text that can be both accessed online and used to create new print copies. This book and hundreds of others are available online in the History E-Book Project through subscription.

Many of the works in the History E-Book Project are available in print and can be ordered either directly from their publishers or as part of this series. For information refer to the online Title Record page for each book. Inquiries regarding this series can be directed to info@hebook.org.

ACLS
HISTORY E-BOOK

http://www.historyebook.org

"You could always tell us unemployed by the sugarbag we carried over our shoulder. It was our badge. They were the sugarbag years."

Front cover photograph from Alexander Turnbull Library. Cover design Jule Einhorn.

"I've been in all the wars," Johnson said, "but I couldn't tell you anything about it."

"You won't talk about it?"

"I couldn't tell you anything even if I did. It wasn't anything. You wouldn't understand it unless you saw it. If you did see it, you wouldn't understand it."

It was very hot and stifling in the cafe, though as we sat there it began to grow quieter, and the smell of fish and cooking-oil was mixed with tobacco smoke.

"I couldn't tell you about the war," Johnson said. "It wasn't a lot different from anything else. I could tell you worse things about the peace."

"What was the peace?"

"That was the bit in between."

"Worse things?"

"Truer things."

And so I said to him, not wanting to move and quite ready to listen:
"Tell me about the peace then."

From 'Man Alone' by John Mulgan

Photo Alexander Turnbull Library.

To my father who saw it. To my son who will never hear about it.

The Sugarbag Years
Tony Simpson

The Sugarbag Years
An Oral History Of The 1930s Depression In New Zealand
Tony Simpson
First Published 1974 by Alister Taylor Publishing Limited Wellington
New Zealand.
Trade distribution Quick Fox-ATP Waiura Box 87 Martinborough New Zealand.

Contents

A Note & Some Acknowledgement

This is an oral history, that is, it is a history in which those who experienced an event—in this case the Depression of the nineteen-thirties in New Zealand—tell their own story. It stands in contrast to the narrative history usually written in which the historian speaks by imposing a pattern on events. As far as I am aware the oral approach is a new one for this country, although it has many followers overseas, the most notable of whom is Studs Terkel, compiler and editor of *Hard Times*, an American view of the same Depression. The approach is similar to that which can be understood by the word 'documentary' although this is, in itself, a misnomer because this book does not use documents as such. It makes no claim to what is called 'historical objectivity' because it relies on memory and experience. It is the genuine voice of a people recounting a community experience from a large number of personal viewpoints.

The material came to me in a variety of ways. By letter, word of mouth either recorded on the spot in note form or immediately after the telling, and, for the most part, by way of taped interviews later transcribed and edited. None of the contributions are acknowledged in the body of the text. Some of the contributors are household names, others are unknown outside their immediate circle of friends, but all have this in common: that they survived a period of seven or eight years in the late nineteen-twenties and early thirties which has etched itself deep into their memory.

Nevertheless, some particular acknowledgements are in order. First of all the influence of Jim Henderson, who taught me to listen to what people have to say, instead of reading what someone thought they said. To Pegasus Press for permission to quote from some poems of A.R.D. Fairburn, Gabrielle Day for permission to quote from *Man Alone* by John Mulgan, to Marion Trotter and the family of the late Jim Forsyth to use extracts from *Return To Open Country* (published by A.H. & A.W. Reed) and to G.P. Davies and Margaret Thorn to quote from unpublished manuscripts. To Nola Neas who transcribed a quarter million words from tape, and to all those people who searched their memories and brought back experiences, many of them painful to recall.

Introduction

My father is dead now these past five years. He wasn't an old man when he died, sixty-three, but he'd always done physical labour and he didn't know how to stop. One day he lifted something too heavy and his heart stopped. His life had been a hard one, measured out in hundred feet of timber from the mill and hundred-weight of coal hewn from the face of the mine. But of one thing he was always certain, and that was that no son of his would ever have to work as he had worked, daily to run the risk of losing an eye to a flying chip or a finger in a railway coupling. It was for this reason that he was a union delegate, and from his first vote to his last he voted Labour. He had a vision of a more just society and when Labour won a great victory in 1935, and again in 1938 after a cruel depression, he was a proud and happy man because he felt that his millenium had arrived. But towards the end of his life his eyes held a puzzled look. He wasn't a leader or a public man, just a rank and file soldier in an industrial army, but had he been able to articulate his puzzlement he would have said, looking about him: "This is not what I meant, this is not what I meant at all." Something had gone wrong. There was no millenium, only war and blighted hopes, the destruction of the militant labour movement in 1951, the dreary fifties, approaching age and the thought of death with not much achieved. His dream was shattered and he could never really believe it or understand why.

He could never tell why because he wasn't able to use that curious abstract language of analysis which is the prerogative of the middle class, and more particularly of its educated "intellectual" segment, for whom he always had the greatest contempt. His view of the world was concrete, influenced by his experiences. The Depression of the thirties was—to him—the apotheosis of the ruling class and the vindication of his own socialist philosophy. It would never have occurred to him that on the contrary it was the nadir of his own hopes for the country in which he and his family before him had lived for three generations, and a vindication, in its effects, of a number of the trends against which he was struggling, and which have come to predominate in our society from then to the present, as they had done in the past. I don't want to suggest that in this his experience was unique, because as a child I had the opportunity to notice his friends, and in retrospect those shadowy figures emerge into sharper focus. Some gave up the uneven struggle and bought a small business, usually a dairy; or set themselves up in their trade on their own account. Most of them prospered, voted National (or if that was too hard a pill to swallow, Social Credit), collected about themselves the paraphernalia of success—a house, car, boat, caravan, seaside bach. And one by one they lost the light from behind their eyes. Others, like my father, were simply puzzled and demoralised. One tiny group descended into a self-destructive bitterness, defiantly clinging to their Marxism and their membership of the Communist Party. Or they stuck to the Labour Party, gathering in cliques to talk of Bob Semple and Mick Savage, suspicious of anyone and anything new, living over and over again the Depression which had—they believed—been both their Golgotha and their triumphant resurrection.

The Depression is part of the folklore of my childhood, a grey and ill-defined monster, an unspeakable disaster, and yet a triumphant major chord. It cast a long shadow, a blight on everything it touched, but it was never recounted in detail. Memories of wasted years, hugged tight to the self and never disgorged—just *The Depression.* My generation, how could we know. You wouldn't understand it unless you saw it, and if you saw it you wouldn't understand it. It was only something which was, and had been experienced, the final word in quarrels: "You'd never think that way if you'd known what I knew in The Depression." All that was left to us was the crumbs of statistics, the gnawed bones of the Barmecide feast, grisly relics of the saints retailed by historians to turn a moral (and a penny) for the present age.

But even from these faint echoes the magnitude of disaster emerges clearly enough for those with eyes to see and a brain to fancy.

New Zealand in the nineteen-twenties and thirties was one monumental cow bail. We lived by exporting primary produce in a very narrow and restricted field. Thus we were very vulnerable to any fluctuation in overseas market prices. Between 1928 and 1931 export prices fell by 40%. There was a consequent fall in government revenue which shrank by five million pounds in 1930 and eight million pounds in 1931—half the total normal revenue. The government was not composed, by and large, of imaginative men. They could see only one answer and that was to balance the Budget by cutting costs. Balancing the Budget became a fetish. In a three-year period public works expenditure was cut by 75%. In April 1931 civil service wages were cut by 10%, and again in March 1932, to be followed by the amendment of the Conciliation and Arbitration Act to such effect that minimum award rates virtually ceased to exist. The only result of such measures was a sudden and considerable shrinkage in purchasing power, and shopkeepers went bankrupt in droves. But this was not an end to government economies. Many were trivial and appeared merely punitive to those who suffered them. Others appear grotesque today. Old age and war pensions were cut by 30%, family allowances abolished, old bandages were re-used in hospitals instead of being discarded, hospital patients' food was reduced and there was a speed-up in the discharge of paupers. It was like trying to bail a sinking boat with a teaspoon—and a bail moreover which leaked the water back into the boat more quickly than it could be bailed out. "It is as if the farmer were struggling in the water", said Peter Fraser in parliament in March 1932, "and in danger of drowning. Instead of the government throwing him a lifebelt or sending out a boat to rescue him, it has decided to throw in the worker to drown along with him."

And drown the worker most certainly did. Prior to the Depression there was no state machinery in New Zealand for the relief of unemployment. There was only a particularly pernicious form of charitable aid greatly reminiscent of the old English Poor Law. It was not a system which could cope with the effects of government policies, for the fall in purchasing power threw thousands of men out of work as the economy rapidly spiralled downwards. In 1930 there were 3,916 houses built in New Zealand. In 1933, at a time when thousands of 'chippies' were walking the streets searching desperately for any sort of work, the number of houses built had fallen to 987. Between 1930 and 1932 the goods available for consumption dropped by 27%. In 1932 the total population of New Zealand was 1,534,735.

The government was finally pushed into some sort of action in February 1931 when they set up a relief scheme for the unemployed. Within a couple of weeks 23,000 men were registered and by June this had risen to 51,000. These men were paid an unemployment rate of twenty-one shillings a week, seventeen shillings and six pence for a wife and four shillings for each child under the age of sixteen. This was calculated by the New Zealand branch of the British Medical Association (not a body greatly sympathetic to the working man) to be quite insufficient to maintain health and working capacity in a normal man. For over two years the number of registered unemployed *males* was in excess of 70,000, rising to an official peak of 79,587 in October 1933. Among the unemployed were 20,000 general labourers, 5,000 farm labourers, and 7,000 building tradesmen. They were the very sections of the population least able to cope with unemployment because they had no resources upon which they could fall back. Nor did the official totals include males under twenty years, or any women at all. At its height, unemployment probably accounted for close to 100,000 workers, or about 40% of all male workers between the ages of sixteen and sixty-five.

Under the various relief schemes there was some work available. But much of it was trivial, non-productive and totally demoralising. The situation was compounded when the Public Works Department sacked all its men and then promptly re-employed them at relief rates, a fraction of what they had previously earned, doing the same work. And as if this was not enough the government pressed on with a form of indentured slavery. Relief workers were hired out to farmers and large companies well able to pay the men a decent living wage, but paying them—on the instructions of the Unemployment Department—the inadequate relief rate. The last straw came in 1933 when the government required at first single, and later married men to go into rural relief camps to qualify for relief. The conditions were primitive, almost barbaric in some instances.

The *Auckland Weekly News* reported thus:

"*The floors of the tents are earthen, uncovered by boarding, and on Wednesday many of them were dampened by rain soakage. The surroundings at No 1 Camp were very muddy. The men bathe in the drains, wash in a horse trough, and if it rains have to don wet clothing next day, for there is no drying room. Men recently arrived at the camp and unused to navvying may earn only five shillings a week, but as they become used to the work and more experienced, their earnings become proportionately greater. There is, in addition, a free issue of candles and soap. Men who arrived in the camp without blankets have been supplied with bedding, which they pay for at the rate of one shilling a week. Damp clothes constitute an ever-present problem at Aka Aka. The men work all day widening drains. Nearly always they are ankle-deep and knee-deep in water, and often waist-deep.*"

In the winter of 1933 there were 45,000 men engaged in straight pick and shovel work on relief. It wasn't much of a life, and the worst of it seemed to be that it had no end. A man on relief could only watch his wife and children starve. There was almost nowhere he could turn.

Between 1924 and 1925 charitable relief for unemployment through Hospital Boards accounted for 455 cases. Between 1931 and 1932 the comparable figure was 18,733.

In 1932 the Christchurch Mayor's relief depot provided 11,000 boots, mostly old ones repaired. There were 10,000 people applying for aid each week. In seven months of the same year the Auckland City Mission doss house provided 37,000 free beds and 102,080 meals.

In 1934 seven out of ten Auckland school children had physical defects, and in the same year a survey of five Canterbury primary schools showed 886 fathers out of work, 225 children suffering from malnutrition, and 618 with insufficient clothing. In 1935 twelve Auckland clergymen of all denominations appealed to the government:

"*Widespread malnutrition in a primary-producing country is nothing short of a national scandal . . . To expect men, women and children to have to depend permanently upon the supply of cast-off clothing is a prostitution of Christian charity to which we cannot subscribe . . . Unspeakable suffering is endured by thousands of honest and respectable citizens who should not be placed in this humiliating position.*"

With the possible exception of Gordon Coates, the government was helpless before such entreaties. They wanted to help, but they could only spread their hands helplessly and shrug. What could they do? They were doing their best. Weren't they? The Budget had to be balanced and there was no help for it. In the event, their best fell far short of expectations.

At the 1935 election the conservative coalition was swept from power in a Labour landslide. By 1939 unemployment was down to 10,000 men on relief—useful government works, not chipping weeds—and the war soon dealt with the slack in the economy. It was all over, at least on the surface.

The statistics quoted are a chamber of horrors on their own but they're only figures, not people. They give an indication of the magnitude of what was happening. What it meant in individual human terms was something different again, and is something I hope you will discover by reading the subsequent chapters of this book. But more generally there is a word for what happened; unfortunately it's an intellectual's word, but one which sums up the experience—it was an existential happening. All the petty social distinctions were swept away, the lies and pettyfogging and humbug. Everybody over vast areas in town and country was on the bare bones of their arses, and there was no pretending otherwise, although some, pathetically, tried to keep up the pretense. It was no good. Old shibboleths failed; the slate was wiped clean.

An existential experience of this sort strikes people two ways. To some it was a liberation beyond their wildest dreams. It is the period of the flowering of our literature such as has been never seen before or since. Fairburn, Glover, Curnow, Mulgan and a host of others. And it was not only poets and novelists who were set free either. There were people for whom it opened up great vistas of social and political action which they had never dreamed possible and seemed now to be in their grasp. But such people were few. Pitifully few. To the great majority of the population it was sheer misery and horror. All their security had disappeared overnight. They didn't want their freedom, they wanted back their security so that nobody could ever take it away from them again. That was what the Labour government was put there to do. No matter what my father was voting for (and it wasn't that, it was far more than that), that was what he was going to get. And he got it.

One by one the creative and adventurous spirits fell by the way. John A. Lee was expelled from the Labour Party, Uncle Scrim was driven away by continual harrassment, the Social Research Bureau was dismantled and in one of the shabbiest episodes in the story of the freedom of the press in this country *Tomorrow* was deprived of paper and ceased publication. Peter Fraser and Fintan Patrick Walsh carved up the Labour movement between them, and a host of lesser unknown spirits (or was it sprites?) became the victims of a new dictatorship, a conspiracy of ordinariness.

Youth, which might have seized the day as was its right, marched off to war and left the field to old men. And the young people came back tired, looking only for a hole in which to hide. Six years of killing was enough for any man. The creative energy and spirit which might have gone into building the new society bled to death at Mersa Matruth or before Cassino. Even the men and women who came back had died, somehow.

Labour became a barbaric parody of itself and fell in the end, tired and old. Fraser's place was taken by Sid Holland, promising a return to the past, the golden days before the Depression. The National victory of 1949 was a communal attempt to wipe out memories of depression and war, to pretend that it had never happened. Holland's first step was to crush what was left of the social conscience of the Depression generation in the great waterfront lockout of 1951. In doing that Holland was not just a wicked man who had somehow gained power—he was a hammer in the hands of a weary community which had no wish to be reminded of blighted hopes. When the militant unions went down to defeat in that epic battle it was possibility which was rolled in the dust.

A dull, grey, suffocating blanket of security swathed the land, the period we call the nineteen-fifties. The Depression ceased to be a cataclysm and became a catechism, a liturgy guarded by old men, a service of exorcism to drive out the demon of criticism. The Depression, which began as an episode in our history, has ended as an element of our national mythology.

Myth is more uniform than history. It is a display of the shared semantic systems which enable members of a society to understand each other and the world they inhabit. A fixed point in a changing universe. In New Zealand the depression has become The Depression, a part of the manner in which we justify the way we act communally. As an event in history it was a community trauma, from which grew a belief in the need for shared solutions. As a mythology the pattern has become its own negative. The state of society is no longer seen in terms of certain consequences flowing from certain events, that is, depression conditions. Instead the Depression becomes the justification for the state of society.

To live through a community trauma, to walk an anxious social tightrope and see many of one's fellows fall is not a pleasant thing. It makes one cautious. Even when one is back on firm ground the habits of careful footsteps remain. The road is plain and sideroads are carefully marked: Here be demons.

For such lack of spirit the Depression must answer, but not entirely. It would be foolish to pretend that there were not certain tendencies in our society prior to the Depression. But what the Depression did was to focus and crystallise certain of these and underpin them in the popular mind with a massive justification. To say that the Depression is a great sustaining myth is not to say that it never happened; it is simply to say that we have forced ourselves to continue to live out for 40 years certain fantasies forged in its furnace.

Many of my informants referred to an incident in which Gordon Coates is supposed to have told a deputation of workers to eat grass. There is no record that he ever said any such thing, and yet many people are convinced that he did say it and that they heard it with their own ears. Whether Gordon Coates ever actually said that or not is unimportant. What is important about it is what it tells us about the nature of communal myths. It is characteristic of myths that they simplify and legitimise. The tale of the workers and the grass is oral tradition. When taxed with it, others who knew nothing of it expressed no disbelief. On the contrary, they said that it had most likely happened. Like most folk-belief it serves to crystallise an abstract and difficult experience. It is a mnemonic, a reminder, a secret sign, and it tells you much about what has been happening in New Zealand since 1935.

But all that was 40 years ago and two generations of New Zealanders have grown up since then. To them history is a foreign country; they do things differently there. I began this book with my father. I could perhaps conclude with my son who may well never hear about it at all. Except that would be unfair to my generation, the people in the middle who grew up repeating a catechism without a revelation. The sins of the fathers, they say, shall be visited on the children. And that is what this book is all about. It is a catalogue, chapter and verse, of a visitation which began the day I was born and continues with me yet.

But I've had my say. Now hear what my father has to tell.

Tony Simpson
August 1973

In The Beginning

As far as the world as a whole is concerned, the Depression is usually attributed to the Wall Street crash in 1929 and that again was attributed to the failure of an Austrian bank in Europe. Now all this thing happened, all this is true. But as far as New Zealand was concerned, the Wall Street crash only accentuated the problem in New Zealand. It began in 1927 and in fact I think it was the fundamental thing that put the government out in 1928 and replaced it by a rather nondescript government called the United Party government. But year after year it got worse. I well remember before the government was put out in 1928 that there was an Unemployment Commission to consider what was to be done about the increasing unemployment. There was no doubt about the falling prices as far as wool and dairy produce were concerned. They had already hit the country and the unemployment was getting very very big by then. By early 1930-31 they'd already worked out and passed legislation for unemployment relief—which we hadn't had in this country before. The development of that legislation had taken place before the effect of the Wall Street crash got through to New Zealand. So in a way we did have some kind of a machine to deal with unemployment, although it was certainly not on the scale that subsequently developed.

From the end of 1926 there developed a down-swing of the slump. This down-swing went past what it was in 1921-22 around about 1929 and by 1930 we really got the additional impact of the 1929 world slump where prices of butterfat were more than halved and the price of wool was 4d. a pound and so on. All this hit commodity products. And it hit colonial countries harder than it hit manufacturing countries. It added to the normal slump that we used to get every few years in New Zealand. We now had this additional world devastation.

So I think, looking back, that the slump lasted ten years and the worst of it was 1931-32 and into 1933. Then very very gradually things started to pick up and I place the pick-up on the depreciation of the New Zealand pound at the beginning of 1933, which added a quarter to the farmers' income, low as it was, and other measures taken by the government—such as cutting interest

New Zealand takes its ease. Prime Minister W.F. Massey (left) "that terrible North of Ireland man", and Leader of the Opposition Sir Joseph Ward, pose for the camera in 1920. Within ten years both were dead, Ward as prime minister in 1929, worn out with old age and trying to cope with the onset of an economic depression he could not comprehend or control. Photo Alexander Turnbull Library.

rates from 5% to 4%, converting the national debt, stopping people from being put off their land and eliminating part of the mortgage that the land wouldn't stand by introducing mortgage relief legislation. I think this all got the farming side going and when the farming results started to come through and trickle into the community, we had the beginning of the uplift, slightly helped in 1935 by rising prices. The shape of the economy was beginning to look right and in addition Gordon Coates of course had set up his Reserve Bank in 1934. This would enable the government to get some money from its own banker, where formerly it had been stopped because the banks were in control and they didn't help the government at all, in fact they made the Depression far far worse.

So we had by 1935 the framework to develop out of the Depression. Then of course the Labour government came in and they knew what they were going to do: guaranteed prices, high social security, full employment, building houses. And this, I would say, by 1936 was the end of the Depression but not the end of unemployment because the jobs had to be made, the people had to be organised into them and money had to be provided. I would say that unemployment didn't finally disappear until the war began in 1939.

It just came on slowly I think. You heard about it from overseas and then it gradually came through to New Zealand and was just the same. There was a falling off of work. I was in the timber industry at the time and there was just a falling away of building and everything slackened up. And most of the other trades, once the building lines started to fall away, fell away with it. I wasn't so bad really, I was the machinist at the time when they were laying off and I used to start at 8am and knock off at three. Then the delivery truck driver used to come on at 10am and work till 5. But the chaps in the yard, stacking and sorting timber and that sort of thing, they were week on and week off, week about. But it was fairly tough while it lasted.

I knew there was a depression on in a vague sort of way, but I was in work so it didn't really affect me much. I knew a few people who were out of work, and it made you a bit more cautious about your own job– getting on with the boss, being careful where you put your feet, that sort of thing. And then I remember in 1931, just before Christmas, the boss came to me and said: "Charlie, I'm going to have to put you off. I'm sorry, but we just can't keep you on, there just isn't the work." It didn't feel much like Christmas after that and when people said Depression after that I knew what they meant. But before I was put off we'd arranged to go down to my wife's parents' place for a holiday, and we went anyway. We thought we might not get another holiday for a while. As it happened I was only out of work for about six months. But that's how the Depression started for me—with a holiday.

There was great rejoicing when the first world war ended. I was only a nipper when it broke out and I don't remember much except gathering acorns for pig food and bottles to raise funds for our soldiers overseas. I remember 10pm closing, but then the celebrated 6pm business came in. The returned servicemen who were farmers or who knew something about farming were assisted and put on the land. Work was about, everything seemed to be going well up till about 1926, when I was taken away from college. My father was in business as a cabinetmaker. After the war he started up on his own and he did quite well for a while. But in 1926 things started to go wrong.

"Gus," he said, "I think we're in for a slump." He'd already gone through one around 1900. "I'm not going bankrupt like Froggy." Froggy was a builder at the time. Dad gave up the shop and started up at home. Things didn't improve, they slowly got worse. They thought they'd better get me into a trade, but this proved useless. Had I gone when I left school it might have been all right, I had a chance to be apprenticed to an electrical trade. Don't forget I was one of hundreds of kids who got left out. Those who were apprenticed were lucky but some were not so fortunate. After serving two or three years at their trade they were released from their apprenticeships and their agreements. Employers were slowly feeling the pinch. Those who could be transferred to other employers were OK, the others fell by the wayside. The bosses couldn't pay them and by 1928 most people who were in business in a small way were going broke.

Dad had money owing to him but it all went by the board, people just couldn't pay. He had to put what he made into the auction mart where it went for a mere pittance. He was trying to recoup some of his losses, and he couldn't let the timber he had on hand just rot. I was working now, I'd been in work for about two years. Bankruptcy was pretty prevalent, although I didn't know it at the time. In North Brighton baches were going up made of packing cases, good solid timber it was. The building suppliers were very concerned and the Council stopped this type of wood for construction purposes. You could buy sections for £5 on very easy terms. I had ideas of buying one myself. My pay at the time was fifteen shillings a week for 44 hours. I was working in a bakehouse labouring and driving a cart, good money, others were getting ten shillings. My mother told me, "Your best friend is a pound in your pocket. Save if you can." I paid her ten shillings board and clothing until I could support myself, half a crown in the bank and half a crown for pictures and smokes.

I was interested in radio at the time and I used to build crystal sets, and in those days if you did that you were called a wireless crank, a kink, not right in the head. To add to my meagre earnings I went out collecting beer bottles on a Sunday morning. Out of those earnings I bought my first suit, £2.5.0. I was on top of the world. The next thing was a bike, that was ten shillings, it took me about two months to get it. Shortly afterwards I was on the breadcart at a pound a week and the promise of a raise in a year. I thought I had it made. I really thought those great old songs of the day: Happy Days Are Here Again, Blues Skies and I'm Looking At The World Through Rose-Coloured Glasses, really meant something. Little did I know that the storm clouds were gathering and I was going to be caught in the deluge in the years to follow.

On the cart my eyes were being opened. I was serving bread in posh areas and I came across the Domestic Help. These kids put in very long hours every day. One night a week off after they'd cleaned up the dinner dishes, and to be back at a reasonable hour, or 11pm if they were going to the pictures. On their night off they even had to be back to serve supper if there were visitors. Wages varied from ten shillings to fifteen shillings a week, in good places seventeen and six. They earned every penny of it. Girls couldn't get work and they were being kept by their parents. Those in service had a roof over their head, and food. Factories were putting off girls everywhere. I was taking stale bread to the relief depots around the city and I can still see those distressed souls.

At Christmas 1929 I had to deliver bread to the pensioners and needy. It was pathetic. I remember so vividly one incident while I was doing this. There was a widow with children, just lost her husband the week before. I knocked on the door, she opened it, and hanging onto her skirt were two little kids. They thought I was their dad, she burst into tears, and that's when she told me all about it. I

IMPORTANT!

A PERSONAL MESSAGE TO YOU

This Circular is issued by the Executive Committee of the Relief Workers, elected by the majority of men on the jobs. Read it carefully and act at once.

To all Relief Workers in Wellington.

Fellow Workers,—

There are thousands of men on Relief Works. Unemployment has grown, and there is no sign that it will lessen to any extent. Relief Works will be a permanent feature of the industrial life of the Dominion. As thousands of men will be permanently on Relief Works, we must protect ourselves on the jobs. Many thought that the present slump was only temporary, that "good times" would come again. For the past three years they have so thought, and now the outlook is as black as ever. This is a move by Organised Labour to join forces with the Relief Workers. Mere "flash-in-the-pan" efforts instigated for political purposes have led nowhere. Permanent class of work calls for permanent form of organisation. The Wellington General Labourers' Union has assisted to form an organisation—the Relief Workers' Section.

On Thursday, October 1, 1931, a meeting of delegates from a number of jobs was held. These delegates represented roughly about 1,500 of the men. They decided to join up in the Wellington General Labourers' Union—Relief Workers' Section.

This organisation is completely self-governing. Not a single penny subscribed to it goes in to the general funds of the Labourers' Union. On the other hand, the Union has spent a fair sum of money on the preliminary work of organisation to assist the Relief Workers to organise. The Relief Workers have full control of their own organisation. The constitution adopted is based on rank and file control, from bottom to top. The basis is the job committee. The job committee shall be elected by the men on the job. Where the job has several gangs, a man from each gang shall be on the committee, where possible, but in any case not less than three or more than five, unless there are more than five gangs. Delegates shall be elected on the job, and shall act as chairman of committee. They shall hold office for six months, unless they leave the job, die, or are removed by a majority vote of men on the job or majority of men present at a general meeting. The delegate shall enrol all members on the job, investigate disputes arising on the job, call meetings periodically to review progress and report to Executive Committee. He shall keep a record of all money paid to him and shall pay same to General Secretary within one week of receiving same from members. Contributions shall be **twopence per working week,** to be paid monthly or weekly to delegate. There shall be no entrance fee. The Secretary of the Labourers' Union for the time being shall be Secretary of the Relief Workers' Section, and the office shall be the office of the Wellington Labourers' Union, thus saving a Secretary's salary and paying office rent. All money paid in by Relief Workers organised in the Relief Workers' Section shall be used, as directed by the Relief Workers themselves, for organising work, as it is only as a combined body, lined up with other workers, that we can hope to win improvements. The Labourers' Union has approached the Alliance of Labour, the National Industrial Organisation, and is receiving its moral and financial support in this effort. In order to build up this organisation and make it thoroughly representative of all Relief Workers, an organiser or organisers, as funds permit, shall be elected at a general meeting to be called for that purpose. Such organiser or organisers, when elected, shall be under the control of the Executive Committee composed of the job delegates.

Intelligent, decent, respectable workers in all other callings have formed Unions. Relief Workers are just as intelligent, decent, and respectable as their more fortunate fellow workers who are in standard jobs.

The objects of the organisation, as adopted by the meeting of delegates, were:—

1. To better conditions of Relief Workers.
2. To take any action calculated to obtain standard rates and conditions on Relief Works whilst they are in operation.
3. To strive for the abolition of the Relief Work system, and work in conjunction with other organisations of workers towards this end, with a view to reinstating men at present on Relief Work, into their customary industry or occupation.

Immediate attention to be paid to the questions of the docking of hours, transportation, change-houses and shelters on jobs, etc.

See your job delegate and join at once.

If there is no delegate on your job, elect one immediately and form your Job Committee. You must act now to prevent further inroads on your conditions. Solidarity is Strength. Join at once. Ask your delegate for further particulars.

Alexander Turnbull Library.

was disturbed all day. I was pretty quiet about it when I got home but I told my mother. "Where does she live?" she wanted to know. On went her coat and she went around to help that dejected woman. If I was looking through rose-coloured glasses I was disillusioned. All I could see was hardship.

I was due for a rise in wages and was told politely that it was impossible, so I was dispensed with. Another was started at one pound a week. It was going on all over the place, people being put off when their raises were due. This was January 1930. By a stroke of luck I got a job in another bakery starting at 6am and doing a small round after I'd finished. I was to help on the new bakehouse, cleaning bricks, making mortar, mixing concrete. On this job I saw the poorer classes, I was amongst the workers. My boss was a property owner, he had houses all over the place. At times I had to collect the rent. People paid what they could.

Scattered all over were the familiar signs: For Sale or To Let. The little shop-keepers were beginning to have a lean time too. They kept open for long hours to try to catch a bob or two. Everybody was saying: "This can't last much longer, things will pick up." Those who had big families were going home to live with their parents. By this method the rent was halved and it gave a little more to spend on food. The single men found it tough—if work came up the married men got the first preference.

Those who were buying a house at this time were having a struggle. They feared losing their job and being unemployed, it gave them cause for alarm, the constant thought of what might happen had their minds in torment. Sooner or later they were faced with the inevitable. Those who were unemployed lost everything. Broke. Returned servicemen were walking off their farms because they couldn't make a go of it. Some families moved to the country hoping to get a day or two of work at a time if it was offered. Around this time the government brought in gold prospecting and Froggy took off down south to make his fortune. He didn't get much out of it except his keep and ten shillings a week. I was paying a pound a week board, my father was getting a day's work a week in a furniture factory. He was offered a half house and a shed for a workshop for ten shillings a week which he took. My pound a week was some help to the old folks whose savings were dwindling. My girlfriend had her pay reduced from fifteen shillings to ten shillings a week, but she hung on to her job. It was better than nothing. She was a housemaid, just a sort of galley slave. We got married in 1930. It was not long after this that I was informed that my services were no longer required. I was replaced by someone else on lower wages. Many firms were not paying the correct wages and when the union got onto them about it the person who complained was in the gun and fired. For me, the crash had come. I was out of work.

People think the Depression started about 1929. Well it didn't. It was different from America where you could point to the Wall Street crash and say: That's when it began. It started years before that. I came out to New Zealand with my husband in 1926. We'd taken a bit of convincing but I had this sister who'd come out here about five years before and she kept writing and urging us and in the end we came. Well, when we got here things were getting bad then. My husband Billy had trained for the ministry in England. He'd given that up but he was an educated man, and he couldn't get work. There was a lot of unemployment. So we said to my brother-in-law: You wanted us out here and told us what a good country it was. You try and get Billy a job. So he came to see us in a few days and he said he'd got Billy a job, and Billy said: What is it, and he said unloading cement from ships. Well Billy just looked at him and he said: I didn't come thirteen thousand miles to work like a navvy. I won't do it. And he didn't. It was a struggle but we got by. Oh, they were hard times.

Nineteen-twentynine is a significant date in the sense that that's when I first had my first measure of insecurity relating to the Depression. I was working, I had only been working for three years, and from office boy I think I got up to some sort of clerk and was just feeling that I was making my way. Then along comes Head Office with its retrenchment policies. Anyone who had not been there for ten years or something was dismissed with sad regrets. So I was out of a job and from then on the pattern followed. I got another job and the same process happened again within two years. I was a clerk and then a tyre salesman and again after a while the London office said retrench, so out I went. I was with Avon Tyres as a salesman, another London crowd, and they too said right, retrench. So I was out of a job again. Looking around, I then got in with a produce merchant and I was selling cheese as counter-lunches round the pubs. We bought in reject cheese from export because the rats had got at it, and our job was to cut out the rat holes, tidy the cheese up and go round and sell it to the pubs at bargain prices. Counter-lunches were still on in those days and in the Depression there were very few pubkeepers who could afford anything else than a bit of "ratted" cheese. Then again, that dried up. Later on we were in this produce firm and we were then offered a deal that if we could go through and prepare a list of our country customers who were not checking their freight accounts, we could make our wages by putting a bit on to the freight. Otherwise we were out on the street again. So we'd get the pattern of small country stores that were not checking their freight and we managed to get some degree of sustenance in overcharging in this way. Of course that inevitably had to dry up because sooner or later there'd be a check back and as far as we were concerned—desperate as we were—it was a distasteful job and as soon as it was possible to get something else I opted out from it.

In the meanwhile of course, we were all young, all ambitious. My overwhelming experience had two aspects: tremendous frustration, tremendous resentment against economic autocracy, old and rat-faced men coming out from England and telling us that we'd got to tighten our belts, take wage cuts, when we had no more notches to take in. And secondly, feeling that the normal things of life, the prospect of marrying, the prospect of exploiting your talent, were not there. It was, in my mind looking back now, an overwhelming experience of passive violence. We felt violence was being done to us in that sense and it was because of that that I understood the meaning and the inevitability of the riots because there were people in a much worse position than I was, although as I say I had no normal prospects—not even getting beer money at the time. There were others . . . soup kitchens—thousands of people were suffering. There was this sense of frustration and tremendous uncertainty and it must have been very intense because it followed me for thirty years. For thirty years I had insecurity dreams. And I'd have to wake myself up and say "Well you're a leading businessman now—you're there—you've made it." Dreams mainly of going round and sitting in interviewing rooms with a lot of people. Dreams of scanning newspapers for advertisements and things like that. But above all, the feeling that we all had—that this was so unnecessary, that it was really a suppression, a passive violence.

At that time we formed a Junior Chamber of Commerce, the first in New Zealand, right in the middle of the Depression. I think my earnings were £2.10.0 when I joined. But from that we started the study of economics. We set up our own debating teams. We at least took positive steps that if the break came, then we were going to ready to exploit that opportunity once it came. We had of course in the process put the wind up the orthodox members of the senior Chamber of Commerce because we were all substantially socialists. Many of us had openly—as we had to—identified ourselves with the Labour movement as being our one opportunity of getting out of this economic stranglehold.

The Depression was greyness. That's a physical reaction. It's the only way that I can describe a sort of hopelessness that seemed to spread around among people who, in the earlier parts of their lives, had been accustomed to security. It was the result of the discovery, a shock really, a discovery that life was not secure any longer. People accustomed to easy living were suddenly without money, or with very little money. They tended to draw in upon themselves, to be rather cagey about other people, to keep to themselves, to not become involved if possible. There was of course a great deal of relief work at a co-operative level but I can speak only of what I sensed among the people I moved among and that was cageyness and hopelessness degenerating into a sort of apathy.

These days I would expect people in their condition to go out into the streets, to march on parliament. I believe there was a march on parliament, but the protest generally was orderly and rather lukewarm. I can remember a big crowd in Latimer Square in Christchurch addressed by Professor Shelley, but it seemed to me at the time to be a rather lukewarm demonstration. It just seemed that a lot of people didn't have the strength to be angry. And those who did have were just keeping to themselves, keeping out of this sort of thing.

There was a man who has become for me a sort of symbol of the Depression. I used to see him in late 1928 driving to work in a little old car. He used to drive it lovingly. I learnt that he was an architect. I don't know how prosperous he was but he seemed to be a man in good circumstances. A year or so later I saw him again in the Reading Room of the Public Library where everybody went to read the newspapers. An awful lot of people couldn't afford to buy papers and men used to go there to read the papers, be warm and to pass the time—to fight the deadliest of all their enemies after hunger—boredom. Here I used to see this man and his clothes were becoming shabbier and shabbier, wearing sloppy old sandshoes and he looked to me the personification of hopelessness; I used to think what a dreary life this poor wretch was having. And then suddenly one day, early in 1935, I saw him again in the Reading Room at the Public Library and he was wearing a new suit and he was looking well and there had been a complete metamorphosis. He was in a new life.

Photo Alexander Turnbull Library.

We were at a place called Kotemaori when the worst of the slump hit. As the railway from Napier was pushed ahead through Hawkes Bay we lived in railway camps at places like Putarino, Waikau, Tutira, Waikare and Kotemaori—which I don't think even exists today as a little railway station or whistle stop. My earliest memory of the slump is that my father was unemployed after the railway was closed down and he was on the dole and taking occasional relief work. We continued there until the Labour government was elected and one of the first decisions they made was to re-open the East Coast line and all the men went back to work and we went from Kotemaori to a place called Raupunga where the viaduct was being built.

During the Depression the government stopped all work on the railway. They simply stopped work—chop—like that. All the men in the railway camps, well, they could either stay there and look for other work in nearby timber mills or on farms or move off—which most of them were very reluctant to do because they were nearly all married. The single men shot through but the married men with families, at least they had a roof over their heads, and they stayed. Everybody knew at that time that it was no use going to the towns.

My father was very morose. Some people think it a wonderful thing to at last have leisure on your hands, but I have never met anybody like this who enjoys not doing anything. Leisure of course is what enables you to do work of your own and pursue interests of your own, but in this particular place the effect on the men was pretty catastrophic as I recall it. They used to go up and sit at the side of the road in a little group and the big excitement would be watching the occasional truck or service car drive past. They would talk. I can recall the names that always came up in talk—there was Forbes and Coates, and of course the great heroes of the time—the ones who were really going to do something for the men—Mick Savage and Jack Lee. Lee was a name we used to hear more often than any of the others.

We were very poor. We never had sufficient food or clothes. There was just my brother and I, but we didn't have overcoats and we used to keep the rain off by taking a sack and pushing one corner into the other and hanging it over our heads as a sort of cape and going to school in the rain that way. We had no shoes, but for footwear sandshoes were the thing because they were the cheapest of the lot—sandshoes without socks. We had two pairs of pants for years—there were the pants that you wore, and your good pants. Your good pants were what you put on when you went to Sunday school or big occasions like that.

I can't imagine how it was that my mother managed. I do recall that things like bacon and eggs were a great delicacy. When there were bacon and eggs in the house it was something that people knew about and looked forward to and talked of with great excitement. I can remember how my brother and I used to have a little competition to see who could make theirs last the longest and we'd sit there and sort of match little mouthfuls and keep it going as long as we could. The old man used to have a garden. He cleared a section of scrub and dug a garden and he was a pretty good gardener and there was always produce from the garden, but meat was always a great rarity. Chaps in this railway camp used to go out shooting occasionally and rabbits and the occasional wild pig would be shared around. If somebody'd shot a pig, word would spread through the village like wildfire and everybody got some. This was the way people used to think in those days—everybody got some.

Bread and dripping was the thing. Butter I think was one shilling a pound and this was a fair bit. I'm not sure but I think dole was fifteen shillings a week or something like that for a married man. Well one shilling for a pound of butter was a fair portion of that. Imagine today spending one-fifteenth of your income on butter! It's quite unthinkable isn't it? So bread and dripping was the thing.

Winter under canvas in an unemployed relief workers camp at Lewis Pass. Photo Frank Renwick.

Photo Frank Renwick.

Although I was conscious of being poor, there were children who were poorer than me, and these were the children of the tunnellers. In Beeby's Fill they used to have to walk to the Kotemaori school. We had a walk of I suppose about 500 yards to school, but these kids had to come three or four miles on foot and they were very poorly dressed—in rags some of them. And even when it was freezing cold, I can always remember these kids being barefooted and always being very cold, their skin was covered with goosepimples and big red blotches, the girls especially. Our school lunches used to be bread and jam. No butter, just bread and jam and a drink of water. I can remember sharing my lunch with the Beeby's Fill kids because they never had any lunch.

Then there was the dole. A little van used to come around and it was on a fixed night, it may have been every Thursday night or something like that, it may have been weekly or fortnightly, I can't recall . . . but you'd hear the toot-toot of the old van up the road. The old man used to get very restless on this particular night. He'd come in and go out and sit around, and then you'd hear the toot-toot up the road. Then it would stop outside our house and toot-toot, the old man would go out and I would go out with him and there'd be a little exchange of banter with the chap who was driving and then the old man would put his hand into the headlight of the van and the coins would be counted into it, and then a little bit more banter and the old man would come inside and the truck would go off down the road and you'd hear it tooting outside the next place. The old man would come in and drop the money in the centre of the table where the lamp was. There was no electricity where we were. He'd drop the money there without any interest in it at all, almost as if he was chucking it away. And he would sit looking at his hand—he'd hold it up in the lamplight and look at it and would say such things as "You know if I could stretch these fingers wide enough I think I could get it round Gordon Coates' bloody neck." Unfortunately, you see, Gordon Coates was Minister of Unemployment and got all this kind of thing because he wasn't in the situation where he, Gordon Coates, could do very much about it. But he was the one who got all the abuse and I know from what I've found out since that Gordon Coates wasn't that kind of a guy at all. But he was the one who got it.

I think my old man was fairly typical. They were all without exception pro-Labour, very heavily pro-Labour. I worked and lived in camps later on where there were two or three eccentric types who were still conservative in those years, but there was nobody like this in the couple of camps I remember of the slump period. People used to look forward to reading the Standard *every week. It used to be flogged around the camp and people would buy it. They couldn't afford very much by way of newspapers, but they always bought the* Standard *and talked about what was in it, and the people and the policies.*

There was an interminable procession of swaggers where we were. There was an empty section across from our house where word must have spread among swaggers that it was a good place to kip. There was a place where they made a fire, there was an old concrete fireplace there, and they used to make a fire and sleep in the "Starlight Hotel" as everybody used to call it at that time. I can remember one Sunday afternoon when my old man was painting (he used to paint in water colours), and my mother was off visiting somewhere. The old man got out his paints and he was painting in water colour and there was a knock at the door and it was a swagger. He asked if we had anything to eat. The old man brought him in and put the tablecloth on the table, set him a place and went to the cupboard. I think perhaps we'd had some meat that day, and I recall him cutting the last of the meat off a bone; there were a few spuds left over, peas and stuff like that. He piled it up, gave the man a bit of bread and this chap ate everything that was put in front of him and thanked the old man

Photo Jim Henderson

and went off down the road. When the old woman got home she went to the cupboard and saw that our tea had gone because this was presumably what we would have had for tea. She tore strips off the old man and accused him of taking food out of the kids' mouths and giving it to some stranger, some bum—well, he sat there and he took it, he never said a single word.

I was teaching at Papanui School and outside workmen were doing something with the drains. It was before Bob Semple came up with his running shoes for wheelbarrows and shovels—and the men were doing that sewer with wheel barrows and shovels. Just outside our windows one man was wheeling a barrow up and down a plank. The children were very interested in this. Well, there was one little boy; he came every day for weeks with a new pencil and I was getting a little bit alarmed. I just wondered what had happened. Pencils were 3d each and we were doing money and time at the time and I said "Well now, wages are half a crown an hour" (as they were then). "How many threepences are there in a half crown?" And there were ten. "So, how long would you have to work to earn a pencil?" And they said, "Six minutes." We got that out by long drawn-out arithmetic, so I said, "Well, now, you look out of that window at that man. He's got to push that heavy barrow and fill that heavy barrow for six whole minutes, you watch him at playtime." So they watched him and then they really understood. I said to them: "Now you understand why you must look after your pencils and things. Every time mother has to hand you out threepence for a pencil, Daddy's had to work hard for six minutes to earn it."

We were right on the bottom rung of the financial ladder. Our real problem was how to look the part, and live at the same time. I think now that we were all square pegs in round holes. The jobs we had required appearance money for us to make a success of them, and we couldn't provide that and live as well. Then the situation suddenly changed. We got, what was for us, the disaster of our lives. The Big Slump.

The first impact was my sister, who arrived home in tears one night to tell us that she had got the sack. The manager had told her he was going to have to close up. This was one hell of a disaster and I didn't know what we were going to do. Mum said not to worry, we'd manage until she got a job somewhere else, but there weren't any other jobs, and we got worse and worse. I knew my turn couldn't be far away, and sure enough I got called in one day and the axe duly fell. Well, this was it. We had nine shillings a week coming in from grandma. That was it.

This slump, in its way, was a great leveller. People whose way of life had been comfortable and easy suddenly found themselves right down with us, and it must have been a frightening experience for them, and in another way, a valuable one. Some astounding anomalies arose during this period. For example, a married man on relief work could not be made by court order to pay his rent, whereas the same man, if in a job, at the same wages—and there were plenty of them—had to pay his rent or suffer eviction. Similarly, no persons with savings could get relief, so the thrifty were penalised, and the spendthrift was the first to get relief payments. The time-payment system had been recently introduced, and many firms had to rent warehouses to store the reclaimed goods from people who were unable to keep up the payments. Numberless insurance policies went down the drain, most of them with no surrender value, and many part-paid sections were surrended to the vendors by the unfortunate purchasers. Many people were literally starving, and some were begging in the street. What happened to some of the old people in this era I shudder to think. Crowds flocked around the newspaper office each day, waiting for the paper to appear, and when it did there was a mad rush to get one and look for any jobs available.

People who had formerly been pillars of respectability soon lost it in the struggle to exist, and I saw tradesmen chipping weeds on street corners and cleaning gutters. This was life with a capital L and it was a case of the higher you were, the further you fell. Down at the hospital, the women stood in queues waiting for food tickets. There were long lines of them and they stood there for hours, some with babies and little tots beside them. At 12 o'clock the clerk would slam down the window and tell them to come back at 1 o'clock, but they never shifted. There were thousands behind them, and to lose your place meant that you wouldn't eat that day or your kids either. It didn't seem to occur to those in authority that a relief clerk for the hour would have helped them. I tramped the town for work and got a job sorting bottles with some Hindus. That lasted a month and the place closed down, so I went on relief, digging a drain at Lyall Bay.

At this stage we were as well off as anyone on our street, which means that we all had next to nothing. My sister had a couple of days a week at the hospital, I was on relief, and we still had grandma. We didn't have the same amount of money, but food got a lot cheaper and we didn't have an image to live up to. People got more friendly too, because the slump had brutally swept away all their little social distinctions. However during this period, we lost poor old grandma. The old lady just didn't wake up one morning. We had to get a doctor, the first time that I could remember. Two of my uncles came round and fixed everything up, paid the doctor and all the other expenses. The funeral was a sad little affair with eight mourners and a few pathetic little flowers. Afterwards

Photo Alexander Turnbull Library.

The start of the Dominion Museum and Carillon, Wellington. Relief workers working on the approaches. Photo Alexander Turnbull Library.

they came back to our place and sat around for a while and then silently departed. Grandma left a vacant place in our house that surprised and disturbed me. I had never taken a great deal of notice of her when she had been there, but her absence seemed to take something away from our home. Mum was very silent for a long time after that, and I think she missed her mother even more than I did. So we lived until fate made another decision for me.

We just jogged along, pursuing our dull little lives and conscientiously trying to better ourselves, but we really didn't have much chance. Nothing ever happened to us, and except for occasional visits from my married sister, our living was flat and uninteresting. Little brother had left school to go on to a farm to work, which was something which astounded me. He was the last person I expected to be interested in that kind of work. However, his very odd letters seemed to indicate that he liked it. I gave him great credit for his forethought, as he confided in me at a later date that he had worked it out that this would be his one chance of saving a few bob. And how right he was. All through the slump he rode it out on the farm, working for practically nothing, but getting three good meals a day. It cost him nothing to live. He never left the farm to visit us, and I think that was a pretty sore point with Mum as she never mentioned him. He stayed on that farm for a long long time and gradually drifted away from the family circle. My sister walked in one day from her hospital job and without any preamble told us she was going to get married. There was one hell of an outburst about this. Mum said she could guess why, which brought a reply that she should be ashamed to think a thing like that, and as a further defence it was proudly announced that the boyfriend was a public servant. What the fact that he was a public servant had to do with his moral character God alone knows, but Mum seemed to have an affinity for the clerical profession and immediately softened.

They duly got married, and that left Mum and me at home. This was starting to be a nightmare, because the rent didn't alter and the gas seemed to cost just the same. Finally we got sued for back rent, but I am happy to say that an understanding magistrate, on examining our position, refused to make an eviction order. Even at that we handed over every penny we could spare to the landlord. We knew that if ever we got financial again, he would ask for the back rent, which after all was only fair.

I started on relief work on a Monday. The pay was fifteen shillings a week for single men, and you were expected to work. We were put to digging a ditch, but nobody knew what it was for or where it was going to. Nobody seemed to know how deep it had to be, so we just stayed in the one place and kept digging until someone came along and moved us on. It was a complete farce, but we were getting paid, and that was all that mattered. I was completely happy there, and I think the reason was that these fellows were my kind of blokes, and I had found my correct social level.

However by this time our position at home had me really worried. It was getting pretty obvious that we couldn't live on what was coming in. Mum was going about with a worried face and I was at my wit's end to find a solution. We thought about taking a boarder, but as Mum rather wittily observed, he would have to pay a week in advance if he wanted to start eating right away. The ditch digging was progressing—to our satisfaction at least—and my two mates, Curley and Big Mac, made the day go pretty quickly with their comments to the poor old foreman-timekeeper who messed about aimlessly all day, and probably wondered why he had been chosen to keep things going. I think that perhaps old Gutsache, as we called him, felt embarrassed at having to give orders to some of the chaps there as there were all kinds of top class tradesmen digging that ditch, from master carpenters through to A grade mechanics.

I had a feeling that old Gutsache and Curley would clash in earnest one day, and sure enough it happened. That clash altered my whole existence. The old fellow strolled up one day and politely asked Curley if he would mind jumping out of the ditch for a second. After a moment's hesitation Curley complied, while we wondered what the devil was going on. When he got out, Curley asked what the trouble was, and the old chap asked him if he would mind raising his foot. Completely mystified, Curley did so and after gravely inspecting it, old Gutsache delivered his masterpiece by informing Curley that he had taken out on that one boot a damn sight more than he had done with his shovel all day. Now Curley, for all his cheek, was a pretty good worker, and this really got to him, but by the time he was ready for a broadside the old chap was well away. He informed us he was leaving, that he wouldn't work with an old cow like that, and when Big Mac sarcastically asked what particular job he intended taking, he was told that he'd see by the end of the week and that there were other things to do besides digging out this junk. So it cooled off and we thought that was the end of it, but it wasn't.

On the Friday Curley arrived, and we gravely presented him with a broken shovel handle as a going-away present. Curley's remark that this was very bloody funny indeed didn't stop us from laughing our heads off. But we changed our tune when he said he had found a job for the three of us which, with a bit of luck, would put us on easy street. Big Mac promptly retorted that one usually got about ten years for robbing a bank, but Curley just grinned and said it was nothing like that, and he would tell us at lunch time. We couldn't wait for it to come. When we were seated Curley unfolded his scheme. We would go gold-mining. It stunned us and we plied him with questions. He had all the answers. He had been to see a member of the Legislative Council and he had all the dope. We talked it over excitedly and it certainly seemed a good idea.

Mum didn't like me going much, but we agreed that she'd move in with my married sister. Then I was away down south. We moved into a mining camp on the Coast and we had a pretty hard time of it for a while. We were pretty green and if it hadn't been for some of the practised miners we'd have been finished. Things got a bit better when the government introduced a subsidy scheme, by which you got a few bob a week to mine if you had a miner's right, because one thing the government really wanted was gold. After a while we started to pick up a few bob ourselves anyway from a patch of ground we were working over.

By then the guardians of our fate (that is the government department who paid us our subsidies) were beginning to take a great deal of interest in our activities, as this subsidised scheme was one of the few that they were getting some return from in the shape of gold sold through the bank. As usual some official who knew nothing about this kind of activity came up with a scheme that to him must have looked pretty good. In short, if a miner sold more than a given amount of gold to the bank in any one month, his subsidy for the following month would be reduced by the amount of extra income he had acquired over and above that laid down by the department. To offset this, the men simply sold enough gold to keep within the subsidy level and sold the balance to private buyers. Thus the scheme succeeded only in driving down the returns to the department.

Some bought a second miner's right in an assumed name and sold the extra gold to the bank or a buyer under that name. The crunch came however when for statistical purposes the Mines Department sent forms to all holders of miner's rights—as they do each year—the holders being required to declare what they had won for the year. Dozens of these letters arrived addressed to people we had never heard of. I could see trouble looming up. It did, and we had a visit from the law. A licensed gold buyer in one of the creeks was interviewed, his buying book temporarily confiscated and he was generally put through the mill. However as he said—and in my opinion rightly so—if some chap came up to sell gold and put his miner's right over with the name Joe Jones, he was accepted as such.

The net result of all this investigation was that nothing really happened. But it was just too much like losing face to withdraw the scheme and it was continued with. It reflected the stubborn insistence which I found in some government departments to refuse to recognise that they can possibly be wrong.

There was a great deal of resentment over this business, and our nearest neighbour, Old Mick, concocted a letter to the department. I read it and it was pretty good. He pointed out that we would have to get some sort of a subsidy if we went back to our various towns, and for the most part it would be paid to us for messing about. Here, we were making some contribution to the economy, so how about leaving us alone to do just that. He didn't get any reply.

Towards the end of our stay we were winning quite a bit of gold and we decided that we'd all go back to my place for Christmas in Wellington. Mum was living at that time for part of the time with one sister who'd married a returned soldier, and the other one who'd married the public servant, and they were very pleased to see us.

They couldn't put us up, much as they would have liked to. There just wasn't anywhere for us to sleep, so that was that. I told them straight out I wanted to know how they were getting on financially. The soldier boy was getting a part war pension for his arm, and the Public Service boy was on relief. Well, I knew what all that meant in terms of money, and it didn't mean much. The soldier boy told me he went before the Board for an increased pension, and soaked his arm in cold water for three hours before he went up to make it look as blue and dead as he could, but he got turned down. Mum's income was a great big nought except for the seven shillings she was now getting from her two surviving brothers. I told them I would make Mum's money up to twelve shillings as long as we were on gold, but if it petered out, then so did the five shillings. Did I think it would peter out? NO—I didn't.

The two husbands were intensely interested in the gold-mining and I could see that they were itching to have a go at it but I didn't encourage them. They had enough problems family-wise to start thinking about that.

I had a hell of a job convincing all of them that they had to look facts in the face, and it started when I invited these two blokes to come and have a drink with us in the afternoon. Both refused, although they both liked a drop. Upon their refusal the fun started. I told them I knew they were broke, and it was a pity they couldn't swallow their bloody pride enough to let their own brother-in-law buy them a drink when he was able to do so. I rather surprised myself as I am not normally the explosive type. After my outburst there was an uncomfortable silence; then the soldier boy spoke. He said he was not used to going in pubs and having somebody else passing over the money for him. It did something to him he said and on reflection I had to concede that he had a point. In the finish, after a lot of argument, with the women chipping in, I lent them a pound each to shout with.

I told the girls I had brought three pieces of gold with me which I was going to get mounted and give them one each and one for Mum. I also asked my sister what Mum was short of and it mostly seemed to be slippers. So I finally left them for the time being and told the husbands where to meet us.

The streets were full of people going nowhere. Most of them appeared to be window-shopping, or waiting for the evening paper to come out. I bought a paper, and from a job point of view it was a dead loss. There were lots of idiot

Photo Auckland Weekly News.

Photo NZ Herald.

Photo Auckland Weekly News.

Pausing in their search for the elusive "colour" to smile for the camera, these are some of the hundreds of men grubstaked by the government at fifteen shillings a week to search for gold. All the gold they panned had to be handed over to the Department of Mines. Photo NZ Herald.

articles about good times just around the corner, but that corner must have seemed a damn long way off to the poor beggars who were right up against it. Everything was cheap but that didn't mean a thing if the money wasn't there. We were glad we were going back and I felt a week would be plenty long enough.

We met up with the two husbands and asked them where they wanted to go. "Anywhere," they said. That suited us as we had no set place to drink in. So they carted us off to a little back bar and we sat down and started to have a few drinks and a natter. I asked them to tell us about how they were getting on generally—what it was like on relief work, and what they did with themselves when there was no work. I was interested to know what the soldier boy did because he didn't work at all. He told us of his efforts and he had certainly been a trier. He'd gone round hundreds of houses wanting to sharpen knives, clean windows, fix taps or anything else that had to be done. He got four shillings out of that lot and he reckoned he'd done 100 miles to get it. While he was convalescing in hospital he had learned fancywork as a therapy, and was apparently pretty good at it. So he got a bit of cheap material and some coloured silk thread and made some ornamental cushion covers which I was assured were damned good. He hawked them around the houses and in and out of shops and finally got a shop to put them on display on a commission basis. He kept going back for months until he got sick of it. As far as he knew they were still there. The other boy spent most of his time trying to coax vegetables from the clay that he had for a backyard. He asked for a piece of ground from the town council, but had no luck there.

They told us about one hotel that put on a counter lunch at midday. It was apparently a pretty good one with cheese on toast, roast rabbit, rissoles and the like. All the old men folk would gather in the bar at 11am and get a handle of beer for fourpence. They would make this last until the counter lunch arrived and that would be their main meal for the day. It was a sort of unwritten law that the old chaps would have first choice and outsiders trying to muscle in were sternly warned off by the barmen until the old fellows were satisfied.

We got one piece of advice from soldier boy which, I thought, showed that he was a considerate person and a bit of a thinker. He told us that if we met any of our friends in town we'd probably feel that the right place to have a yarn about old times would be the pub. He advised us to first ask them what they were doing, and if they were on relief, not to suggest it, as they would be broke, and it would only make them embarrassed. He was right of course, and it was something we hadn't thought of.

We finally left the pub and were invited home to tea. We knew this was just a friendly gesture, but we accepted with the proviso that we buy it. We bought a mighty bundle of fish and chips and arrived home with it, a bit the worse for wear and with numerous bottles stowed away on our persons. I shot around and got my other sister and we had an all-in meal.

We went back down south again after about a week. It'd really knocked us back to realise we thought we had it pretty rough, but that we were living in clover compared to the people in the cities.

I remember, too, not long after we got back we had a visit from some officers of the department who addressed us and made a long speech about nothing in particular. They asked us if we had any complaints to make and whether there was anything we thought was needed. I never ever understood why they came but concluded it must be the first faint shot for the forthcoming election. Well we had plenty of complaints. We wanted a library, we wanted medical assistance or at least a first-aid cabinet, and we wanted a telephone number arranged for us to ring in a medical emergency.

But if anyone got up to speak, this bloke would ask his name and then look up a list and tell the speaker how much he owed the department in subsidy paid. This enraged the diggers to a point that one bloke who was a bit of an orator got up and said he wouldn't give his name until he had finished what he had to say. In between other things he told this chap that he didn't owe anybody anything, and did he consider that he owed the department what he himself was getting. He also pointed out that this was one of the few schemes the department had which was giving them any return. He pointed out our extreme isolation and the primitive conditions under which we were living and finished by saying that they should be grateful for the fact that we were down here doing our best to retain our self-respect and not causing any trouble like some groups were doing. The old gentleman was so astounded that he didn't even ask him his name but ended up by promising to look into the points we had raised and would in due course advise us what had been done through the paymaster. We never expected to hear from him again but to our astonishment we did get a first-aid cabinet and a small collection of books. But we never got that number to ring for medical help. However we'd not done so badly out of that little visit, although the reason for it remained an unsolved mystery.

I was living at Rakaia during the Depression. There wasn't any work of course, except relief work and that was just no good at all. I think I'd have rather starved. So some of us got together and we decided we'd work for ourselves.

We used to stretch a length of wire netting across the Rakaia river bed. About four or five hundred yards wide. You know what those river beds are like. Very wide. Not much water but a lot of shingle and broom and stuff. Riddled with rabbit burrows. You could just about watch the ground move. I've never seen so many rabbits. Then we'd get about a mile up the river-bed on horseback and we'd ride down towards the netting cracking stockwhips and the rabbits would take off up the river-bed and a fair percentage of them would always run straight into the wire netting and get themselves tangled up. Every now and then we'd get a wild cat in the netting too. We always had a hell of a time getting them out; they used to fight like demons, clawing and spitting. Well anway we'd get those banana boxes with the two parts to them and we'd put a live rabbit in each one and then we'd throw in a turnip. We got them cheap from the farmers. Sometimes we'd pinch them but usually we'd buy them. Or be given them. The farmers couldn't sell them anyway. Then we'd nail a lid on the box and take them down to the railway station and send them to Feron's in Christchurch. By the time the rabbits had eaten that turnip they'd be the fattest rabbits in New Zealand. I think we used to get sixpence each for them. It wasn't a bad living and you were in the open air. Better than some.

I was on the dole in Hokitika for some time and it was a pretty hopeless situation, and I got a job up near Otira at one part of it and finally that closed down and we were back on the dole again. And I happened to be in Greymouth and an aunt of mine—she had some friends round the town, they were building a new theatre there, the Regent theatre. She came home and said, "I've got a job for you and Dave," that was her son, my cousin . . . And just inside the entrance of the half-constructed brick theatre, there was a big pile of gravel and the foreman would say to a couple of his men, "Right, grab those two shovels, here shovel that heap of gravel over there will you . . ." And some of the poor wretches hadn't worked for two or three years, probably good workers some of them too, but they get fairly soft after a long spell of inactivity . . . And he'd stand there watching them for about five minutes and then in most cases he'd say, "Hey, you're no good to us, go up the office and they'll give ya half a crown."

The next two would have a go, but we made the grade for we'd been actually working hard up to about a week before and we got a job up on top of the scaffolding. The cement was hauled up by barrows and we stood on a platform, and as the wet cement barrows came up we'd unhook them onto the platform. We'd take turn about. Another barrow'd come up and off we'd go along the scaffolding, and it was rickety and it had no protection.

However, we got used to wheeling round these barrows of cement hour after hour, and on particular big jobs they'd keep us on three or four days. Well, the biggest job we ever had was a great beam right across the width of the theatre. I think it might have been about ten feet deep, it'd be about 6 feet wide and quite a long way across the full width of the theatre. Well that had to be completed in one day.

We had to start about four in the morning. I think we ended about two the next morning flat out. About two or three in the afternoon my hands started to become raw with the grabbing hold of the wet tackle and the rasping of the wet cement and started to burn. By four o'clock they were dripping blood as I was wheeling backwards and forwards.

Finally there was a trail of blood right along the gangway to the big place we were filling in. Well, round seven or eight o'clock at night I was just about delirious with pain and apart from fatigue the pain was terrible. And the burning. It was agony. We were actually grasping these wet cement handles and the blood was rushing out. The skin was all raw. You can imagine the pain.

And I stuck it out. I was half silly with pain when I got home. Went to the doctor next day and he said, "Where on earth have you been?" And I told him. He said, "Oh my goodness, you can't go to work for a few days."

And I'm pretty certain there was no compensation. That was the finish. He gave me instructions what to do. I think it was more a matter of time than anything. The cement had caked up with the blood and I had pretty hard hands for a day or two till it gradually disintegrated in the warm water.

Well that particular foreman he was round that building watching the workmen—like a squirrel—he'd been all over the show, and the men were actually afraid of him every time he went round. A lot of them resented it too. And the carpenters were workin' so fast their hammers bangin' with almost machine-gun rapidity—everyone was going flat out.

One day when Dave and I were up on the scaffolding which was about fifty or sixty feet above the ground, wheeling the cement around, we'd been going flat out for a few days and doing a good job evidently, this foreman came along and said to me, "Do you think you blokes could run with the barrow?"

I said, "NO! No, I don't think we can run with the barrows."

He just walked away. I expected him to say I'd have to go but no fear he kept us on.

Well I nicknamed him Simon Legree and on one occasion—I think it's the only occasion after we'd done a big job—we all went down to the pub to have a few beers after the job was over, and he happened to be standing near to me while we were havin' a yarn, different fellows, and he said to me,

"Hey, Dan, I believe you've nicknamed me Simon Legree?"

And I said, "Yes, that's right Jack."

He said, "Who in the hell was he?"

I looked at him and said, "The bastard who flogged Uncle Tom to death."

And he gave a shocked look and never said another word.

The Poor Get Poorer

We were a family of three children. I was the eldest and there was a brother at about two-year intervals. We were middle-class people on a middle-class income. I got work first as a storeman and then as a serviceman. Around 1929 I was sacked from the job as being the last person on the staff. The best my father could do was to feed us and clothe us after a fashion. We were never actually hungry, but there wasn't a sufficiency of food as there had been previously and for a period—about eighteen months—I worked at all kinds of jobs like teaching people to drive motorcars, picking green tomatoes at a pound a week six days a week eight hours a day, that sort of thing. Everybody could make some kind of effort and contribution. It was the kind of thing that could happen in any particular area and to any people. In Addington, Christchurch, somebody would save up enough money to buy a packet of carrot seeds and these would be spread among seven or eight homes, you know, a pinch of carrot seeds to each home, and people who had the energy cultivated these things so they would have some fresh vegetables. They couldn't afford to buy any.

The results of the Depression on some people were very distressing. I can recall a person who was the head man in the primary school which I went to. His people had a little business but because he couldn't get any work—and he was out of work a lot, longer than I was—he took to thieving and finished up in jail. He had a mind which was much above this sort of thing but the general Depression had many effects on a whole lot of people. I had a cousin who was a steward on the ferry between Wellington and Lyttelton and about once a week to make sure that I had at least one decent meal I was invited down into the crew's quarters and had a meal. And I'm quite sure that at that time the Union Company was feeding about two or three times its normal ship's personnel, if not for several meals a day, at least for one meal a day. There were an awful lot

In Christchurch they instituted the "pound" scheme. Each street was requisitioned by volunteer canvassers who collected a pound of foodstuffs from each household for the relief depots. Photo Auckland Weekly News.

of people standing round the streets and smoking in doorways. At eighteen years of age and a fairly long time ago it's difficult to recall but I know that it used to shock me a bit. People standing in doorways . . . waiting . . . waiting . . . waiting. You'd see the same people there day after day just sort of hoping that jobs would come along. I think it was in 1932 or 1931, that's right, when the Broadcasting Company was changed over to a Broadcasting Board and round about the end of 1932 we had an election and this was the period in which there was a march of people on Parliament and they were told to eat grass.

We were living in Bell Hill during the Depression. My husband had a job in the mill—he was never out of work so we were lucky. But they brought some men into the district. The government was paying them about five shillings a week to pan gold in the creeks up the back. All the gold went to the government, they didn't get any of that themselves, although I think some of them used to keep a bit back. The poor beggars were living on boiled potatoes. That's all they could afford. The wives at the mill used to club together and put in a few pence each now and again and buy them some tobacco. It wasn't much, but it was something.

We moved to Christchurch later on. People used to walk over the hills to Lyttelton, about thirteen miles in some cases, just to catch a fish for something to eat. They wouldn't go to Sumner much. It was nearer but you had to pay a penny to get on the pier to fish and they couldn't afford that.

Or they'd go out to Marshlands. There were great heaps of potatoes just rotting there. The farmers couldn't sell them but they wouldn't give them away either, but most of them didn't mind if you nipped across the fence and helped yourself to a couple of pounds. The farmers looked the other way anyway.

There was this lawyer who was a war cripple and he could hardly walk. His law firm failed and they sent him out on relief work somewhere close to where he lived. Well. he was working one day and someone came and told him that the bailiffs were into his house loading all his furniture onto a truck. He said he wasn't going to stand for that so he hobbled off home with all his mates from the relief gang and when they got there they just started unloading all the furniture again and putting it back in the house. So pretty soon there was this mad game of chasing going on with people climbing in windows and the bailiffs fighting a losing battle, and when somebody slammed down a window and broke a bailiff's fingers they decided they'd had enough and they just got into the truck and drove away and all they got was one sewing machine. Being a lawyer this fellow wasn't going to put up with that so he started writing letters saying he wanted his sewing machine back and the correspondence went on for thirty years about that sewing machine until eventually the lawyer died.

Just after I left school I was lucky enough to get a job with these Italians who sold produce door to door and I got a few shillings a day. It lasted quite a long time this door to door selling. A shilling's worth of potatoes at a time or tomatoes. Even a forty pound case of tomatoes you'd sell for about a shilling or two shillings. You'd pay about fourpence or something down at the markets. I can remember one time down at the markets where they let you have them for nothing if you paid the price for the cases, just to get rid of them. We were a bit cunning in those days because there were a lot of government employees, especially in Hataitai, and they got paid once a month. We knew exactly what their payday was and we'd go around the next day and make a few sales that way.

We saw a lot of hardship. There seemed to be despair, unhappiness, a general despondency. People were wondering what they were going to do . . . apart from those who had regular employment with the government; it also actually made for a lot of bitterness amongst people.

I can remember that the Forbes and Coates government was extremely unpopular then because there was a saying that Coates had said: Let them go to the Basin Reserve and eat grass. Whether that was true or not I don't know, I didn't hear him myself, but that was the saying. It wasn't a happy time for people.

I missed some of the early days of the Depression because I had been a couple of years abroad doing post-graduate work and when I came back to New Zealand at the end of 1932 I was a Doctor of Philosophy and had all my qualifications. But all this made no difference—there was no job for me. I had been a teacher but the view was taken that I hadn't enhanced my qualifications by being abroad; I had missed out on teacher training and there were many quite able teachers who were unemployed and working in unemployment camps and therefore there weren't any openings. My family all were unemployed—my father and my brothers and my elder married sister and her husband. My father, who was a highly skilled craftsman, had been given a job two days a week raking leaves in Central Park. You can imagine what this must have done to his proud craftsman's soul. It was only in later years that I realised how degrading and how terrible this must have been. But of course we had had unemployment in New Zealand in the years before and my father had been off work. But to come back to work of this degrading, soul-destroying nature was something really that I don't think any human being should be asked to put up with. My elder brother had also been trained in the building tradition. He was a highly skilled craftsman in the plumbing, tin-smithing, metal-working area and he had been unemployed for three years. His marriage had been delayed because he lived at home and he couldn't get married. I think that he probably managed to keep out of an unemployment camp as a single man and therefore he didn't get any relief and scratched about ten shillings a week out of odd jobs he did for landlords who wanted to repair the spouting or do something about maintenance on an old house. And he had such a job, lasting about two days or a week when I came back home. He said to me "Why not share this job with me? You're unemployed. Be my assistant." Well, I'd been brought up in the building trade and so my first job on coming back after my post-graduate work and all the qualifications I had, was to be a plumber's assistant. My job was to take the soldering iron up and down the ladder, clean out the muck from the spouting, take all the dirty work away and service the skilled tradesman that my brother was.

This went on for a short while and then after Christmas while I was still unemployed, I was offered a job by Mr Downie Stewart who was Minister of Finance, as an expert in economics and taxation. A Treasury job. But very soon Mr Downie Stewart resigned and in his place in a few months Mr Coates took over as Minister of Finance and I was hired by him as a temporary public servant and from then on I at least had a job. So, from my personal point of view, I didn't suffer much. I was young. I lived at home. My mother through hard work had managed to pay off her mortgage and this was the thing that saved us. And we had bread and butter, vegetables, and occasionally some meat.

My young brother had managed to get a job helping a vegetable hawker and this meant that he could catch a few odd tired vegetables and bring those home too as part of his pay. We scratched of course, but our living standard was much higher than many of the people with whom I had gone to school.

There is one incident I will never forget. When I came back to my suburb, one of the boys who had been to school with me said "We'd love you to come home to our place. We haven't seen you for years and we'd like to welcome you back." I went to his place and there were no carpets on the floor, they'd all been sold, instead they had potato sacks. The table had no tablecloth, it was bare. They had some plates, they had no saucers. They brought out half a loaf of bread and this was the welcoming meal for me and they said "Bill, we have saved up some butter." And I cried. I cry now. I'll never forget the welcome that this man gave me—this tremendously emotional thing that he'd saved up a bit of butter and starved to give me a welcome home. Now, that's the kind of thing that I saw in the Depression. Human beings helping each other. Humanity coming through, and yet the official organisation being completely unable to cope with this enormous economic and social blast that had hit the country.

People were charitable. People were collecting stale pies from confectioners' shops and vegetables from grocery shops and various public organisations were asking grocers to give this and give that and there were people who would come to these centres where the goods were collected and queue up to get perhaps a couple of old pumpkins.

I saw many of the effects in human terms of unemployment. The delayed marriage for example. Now this meant of course very great strain and unhappiness but it had also its effects on our population. Population started to go down and the graphs of population that I used to keep in my office for the Minister of Finance showed that the population of New Zealand would fall, not rise. This

Men and boys chop kindling on relief work August 1932. Photo Alexander Turnbull Library.

was one broader effect and what effect that had on people's homes and home life was terrible. Young men and women who should have gone ahead making their own homes were crowding in with their parents and their parents being unemployed were in turn trying to crowd back into their parents' place and you had a very great overcrowding of homes, at a time when houses were empty because people couldn't pay rents. Now this social over-crowding was a very very bad thing which people haven't noted enough as being a cause of great social distortion. There were of course other things of a general nature that one noticed, for example many men, middle aged and older, who had nowhere to live, no ability to pay rent, would make a little nest for themselves just as a rat makes a nest, or a bird makes a nest, in the hills around Wellington—on the Tinakori Hills or on Mount Victoria. They'd get into the base of some tree and get pine needles and leaves and branches around them and gradually collect old overcoats from the relief agencies. They'd get around town with these ragged clothes, partly protected by newspapers, and they would live a life such as they could. They would sleep out at night and then come in to one of the soup kitchens and get a bowl of soup and gradually live through the years.

Many of these people did not come back, they just stayed down and out. They got into the habit of living like that and coming back and renewing their morale was one of the most difficult things. And of course they'd been out of their skills for many years. Now these weren't what we normally might call hoboes today. They could well be a cross-section of people of all types. The impact of this lack of skill and lack of morale is still showing through in New Zealand—this worrying about the future, this lack of confidence, it's still with us.

There are other things that happened of course that are of a very broad nature, such as the fact that we didn't build enough houses because there weren't people to pay the rent. We didn't go on with our public works because the taxes weren't there to pay for them. We couldn't borrow, so that things like hospitals and schools, roads and bridges all went and it took years to make this up. The blow that this all was to New Zealand economic and social life hasn't been measured but it was very great indeed.

The Rich Get Richer?

I knew a fellow during the Depression who came from quite a wealthy family—his father was a doctor, but I think the family had private means as well, and they weren't doing too badly. This fellow was a medical student, following in father's footsteps as many of them do. Well, for some reason he fell foul of his father and the father, traditionally, cut him off without a penny. But this fellow was determined he was going to be a doctor and he wasn't going let a little thing like no money stop him. In those days of course the universities were only really for the wealthy, and don't forget this was in the middle of the Depression. He couldn't get a holiday job or anything like young fellows do today. With thousands of men out of work there just wasn't a chance. This student had a small allowance from his mother and that bought his books and his microscope and paid his fees but that was all. So he got to know all the caretakers just about in Dunedin and they'd let him sleep in the basements of buildings on a pile of sacks, or he might have had a blanket, or even wrapped himself up in old newspapers, which are quite warm. He chose basements because in those days a lot of big buildings had a furnace down below for the heaters and in the winter it would never really go out, and I suppose he'd bed down close to the furnace and it would keep him warm at night. And he got to know a lot of the restaurant owners and publicans and he had a sort of beat worked out. They knew his problem and he'd go to as many as he could in rotation, one a night, and wash dishes and they'd give him a meal. And this went on for several years, however long it took him to finish his degree. And eventually he

THE PIED PIPER OR "MUSIC HATH CHARMS."

graduated. I don't know what he did when his clothes wore out. Probably gave up wearing socks and shirts or something or other. He was quite a legend down there at the time. And then he went away to the war and was killed only a few years later.

I suppose we were very well off indeed during the Depression compared with most people but it's all relative really. We thought it was a terrible thing when we had to let the maid go. My parents that is. And they kept on only the part-time seamstress and the washerwoman. We thought we'd really come down in the world. And when we were told we could have either bread and butter or bread and jam but not bread and butter and jam, because times were hard, we thought it was the end of the world. But don't run away with the idea that things weren't bad for my father, or that he was an inhuman capitalist. He owned a lot of property in the town where we lived but he lost a lot of it too. He just wouldn't collect his rents. He used to say: "The poor buggers can't pay, so why try and make them. At least it's a roof over their head and even if I evicted them where would I find anyone who could *pay the rent." So he couldn't meet all his commitments and he lost out in the end. Depressions affect the whole community, not just poor people.*

I was in the motorcycle business. I had a motorcycle agency and we were selling almost all of our motorcycles on hire purchase terms—about 25/- a week payment, something like that, and as the Depression got worse and especially as farm labourers' wages came down, of course farm boys couldn't afford to keep up the payment of 25/- a week on a 5/- a week wage so we had increasing numbers of machines either thrown back at us or we had to repossess them if they weren't brought back to us voluntarily.

Things came to a head in 1932. All the machines that we had thrown back had of course no payments coming in from the hire purchasers, and the finance company we were dealing with looked to us to make the payments. As soon as a machine came back we just paid the finance company the balance that was owing on it and the machine then became our property. But that wasn't very much satisfaction because things were so bad there were no machines selling. It was almost impossible to sell a motorbike and sometimes we'd have a machine returned to us half, two-thirds, three-quarters paid for and we couldn't resell it for the balance that was owing. At one stage the finance company was very concerned about the way things were going, and we gave them a debenture over the business and sometime, I think about September or October 1932, they took action under the debenture and took over the whole business. I can remember my feelings when a representative of the finance company came and said that he'd been sent to take the keys of the business from me (keys of the safe and everything) and as a result of that I walked out of that business without a penny. We had a little house and we lost that—the mortgagee took that. We sold what furniture we had to pay off our debts and I was completely ruined. We didn't go bankrupt, but we certainly went into liquidation and for several weeks I went around in a daze. I had no income. I had a wife and a couple of kids. We had no money. I used to sit in the office of my brother's shop, only semi-conscious. I remember on one occasion—he probably didn't realise how serious the situation was—on one occasion he said to me "Have you had anything to eat today?" and I said "No". And he said "Well, if you look in the top righthand drawer, I throw all my odd threepenny bits in there, help yourself." I opened the top drawer and there were five threepenny bits in there. Things were so bad I wasn't too proud to take the five threepenny bits. Then, later on, we were literally starving, and I went to the Auckland Hospital Board's offices in Kitchener Street, and they gave me an order for two weeks' grocery supplies on a grocery firm.

Just about at the end of that time an acquaintance of mine in the motorcycle business came to see me in my brother's shop; he'd been looking for me and he said he was looking for a motorcycle and sidecar and he wanted a game of tennis. He said that if I could beat him the best of five sets of tennis he'd give me an order for a motorcycle and sidecar. I had an arrangement with most of the motorcycle dealers who were still in business, and in particular with the company who'd taken over my old business, that I was to get 10% commission on any sales I put through. I beat this chap at tennis and he gave me an order for a motorcycle and sidecar and I got sixteen pounds as commission, and that was very welcome. It gave me a bit of courage to start off again and I looked round for more premises and I found an old stable in Rutland Street. The premises were owned by two elderly ladies and I saw them, told them the story and asked them if they would give me two weeks' credit for rent, which they agreed to do because premises were hard to let. I went to the advertising managers of the two newspapers who had lost a little bit of money—unpaid accounts when we went out of business. They were sympathetic and we made an arrangement that I was to have a limited amount of advertising credit and if at the end of the month when the account was due I couldn't pay, any further advertising that I wanted to do had to be on a cash basis, not on a credit basis. This is how I started. I couldn't even afford to buy a cash book to keep cash in and out, and I took one of my daughter's exercise books and tore out the pages that had been used. I still have that right here, this book is a very cherished document. I opened up the new business on Monday 30 November 1931 and the first entry in the book is *Cash in Hand: 3/-½d.* That was the capital I had and the first and only money I earned on that day was a shilling delivering a parcel. My brother had come along and he had a parcel that he wanted taken to the railway station and he said if I wasn't busy would I take it down to the railway station for him, and he gave me a shilling for my tramfare. Well, I needed that money so badly I walked all the way from Rutland Street down to the present Auckland Railway Station and back. And that was the first money I earned. I had an old motorcycle that I used for running around on that was my only form of transport, and I spent my ill-gotten gains on morning tea 1½d, a gallon of benzine 1/11d, and vegetables for home 10d. So that amounted to 2/10½d out of my 3/-½d. So the following morning I had twopence. I had an arrangement that I would buy a buttered bread roll and a cup of tea and that was what I lived on. So that was all the food I had that day. And this happened for weeks. Then the next day I sold a motorcycle on commission for a motorcycle dealer, and I got 30/- commission and I spent that. I had some business cards printed that cost me 10/-, morning tea 1½d, groceries for home 2/8½d, vegetables and fruit 1/11d, a *Star* 2d, an advertisement in the *Herald* for a machine that I had for sale 1/-, some nuts 2/6d, and then—luxury of luxuries—I shouted myself to supper and spent twopence on it. And that amounted to 19/7d, leaving me 10/7d for the following day. It went on for weeks.

We learnt some terrible lessons—the lessons of mutual aid. Even when we were starving ourselves, if we had a couple of bob we'd lend it to somebody who was worse off than we were ourselves. The Depression taught us the value of money; we learnt not to waste anything, to do anything. It was cut-throat, it was murderous. Many and many a day and night I'd gone round literally starving, with that empty, hungry feeling. And my wife and my kids at school of course, I don't know how they felt. I tried to provide for them as much as possible. I lived on this buttered bread roll and cup of tea, and sometimes 2d. for supper (I don't know what I bought for 2d, maybe a sandwich), I lived on that for about two weeks before I could afford to get something better. Of course we knew of other people who were even worse off than we were. At least we had a roof over our heads and we were protected from the elements, but it was a terrible experience.

It was a bad time for businessmen and I suppose it killed some of them. It killed my father. He was watchmaker and jeweller in Rangiora and of course people brought their watches in to be repaired, but they didn't have any money to pay for the repairs, so there was no money coming in. And my father wasn't the sort of man who liked to worry my mother with money matters, and he mortgaged the house so he could go on giving her the same housekeeping money she was used to. He didn't want to worry her so he mortgaged the house to give her money. And of course there was still no money coming in and eventually the bank foreclosed on the mortgage. It was the end of the world for him, he was very respectable and he'd never been in debt and it hit him like a blow in the face. He just more or less curled up and died; he had a stroke and died. And that's when my mother found out that he'd mortgaged the house, and she said she'd much rather have had the bit less in housekeeping to make do on than lose the house. But then it was too late and she lost the house and actually rented a room in the house she'd thought she owned, to have somewhere to live herself. It just about broke her heart too.

A lot depended on the strength of the local people in seeing that their unemployed first of all got sustenance and second got work. You could get I think it was two-thirds or three-quarters of the cost of building a house from the government if you put up the rest. I could show you a lot of houses down in Karori West at the back of the Karori school on the hill which cost four hundred pounds each, four-bedroomed houses, the builder got the rest from the State. The Prudential Insurance Company building down on Lambton Quay too. Prudential sent one million pounds out here; they got quarter of a million extra straight away on the exchange basis and they put that building up and they got two-thirds of the cost of the labour on that building from the unemployed funds, which was a net profit. They built the building and had about a million and one hundred thousand left over.

Lots of people did very well. The government subsidy for labour was very sound, it was a very sensible thing, but what happened was this. The great thing was to get jobs organised which were profitable in the sense that they were productive, not digging holes and filling them which is really what happens. If anybody could stump up, I think it was a quarter or a third of the cost of a building, the wages (not the material but the cost of wages to the tune of whatever the percentage was) came out of unemployed funds. Now that meant that if a contractor had enough money to start with and a bit of land, he could get the rest of the wages paid from the Unemployed Workers' Bill and the carpenters, plasterers etc were employed at full rates of pay and that was much better than having them on unemployed workers' relief. Well, the Prudential in Wellington was the best example I know of a big dramatic building built on this basis. But that wasn't the only one, there were lots, I know that. A tremendous lot was done in rural areas. Farmers who had a little bit of capital and who could get hold of a bit of money, could get all sorts of improvements and work done. They could get sheds built and fencing done and swamps and all that sort of thing done out of the unemployed relief. And this was sound. The government should have done the same sort of thing in teaching instead of putting on ration teacher system where you got one term's work for twelve pounds a month or something. It would have been far better to have paid them and reduced the size of classes. It would've put money into circulation. I mean, the deflationary trends of the Depression could be negated only by an inflationary trend surely, and the thing to do was to put people to work at full rates of pay in their job wherever that was practicable. It was very difficult to do and created a lot of fuss. One thing is that the solid trade unionists who weren't out of work weren't all that happy about it. But it was possible if you could hold on. For instance some farmers did. I know one farmer in the Wairarapa who held his wool for four years in the Depression and then sold it when the prices came right—they made money. Contractors who had money or could get money and could use it shrewdly and get labour paid for them, they did very well. But one can't be against them, because they had men at work.

In 1931 the Chairman of Directors of the Dominion *was a Mr Hugh Williams of Lansdowne, Masterton. He had an Oxford MA degree and he lived in an English-style manor house with spacious grounds but was well known for his meanness, to the point of notoriety. Having returned to New Zealand the year before, after a 30,000 pounds spending spree in which he and his wife had purchased antique furniture and other furnishings, including a concert grand piano which neither of them could play, they proceeded to furnish their newly built house at Lansdowne. Unfortunately wool prices had dropped after their home was completed and economy was the order of the day. Williams summoned the manager of his station from some twenty miles out of Masterton to discuss reducing the manager's salary. Prior to the manager's arrival Williams set the stage well. He had his large Rolls Royce put up on blocks in his garage and he purchased a "biscuit box" Austin, the forerunner of today's Mini. When he found he couldn't fit his portly frame behind the steering wheel he had the front seat taken out and an enlarged back seat was made to replace the original front seat. When the manager arrived Williams explained the great economy that he was making in his own motoring expenses by storing his big car and using the little one. Then he told the manager that a substantial cut in the manager's salary was necessary. The manager demurred at the size of the cut, so Williams asked him to come for a drive and they could discuss the salary as they drove along.*

"You see," said the manager as they drove along, "I'd hardly be receiving any more than the station hands, and think of my responsibilities Mr Williams."

"Yes," replied Williams, "I see. But there's an answer to that." He then headed the car out to the station. When they arrived Williams summoned all the station hands. Thinking they were all about to be fired the men lined up apprehensively. Williams spoke:

"Well men, times are hard. But none of you need worry. I'm not going to sack any of you. You'll all get three meals a day and a roof over your heads as long as you work hard for me. But for the present, while times are bad, there'll be no wages for any of you."

With that, Williams dismissed the relieved station hands with a wave of his podgy hand and walked back to the car with his manager. "There you are," he said. "You can't complain now. See how lucky you are to be still receiving a lot more than your men are. And remember that the car I supply you with for the station is much bigger than the one I'm forced to drive around in now."

While the manager was thinking all this out, Williams—sitting in the back seat of his converted car—disappeared in a cloud of dust down the road to Masterton.

The Man On The Land

You could see it looming up. Everything seemed to be at a standstill. New Zealanders really struck it. The country wasn't moving at all, there was no talent in the country at the time. I hope you don't mind my saying this because I'm just speaking as I found it when I came here. And so, yes, we went to Christchurch and were there four months and my husband had difficulty in getting established and finally he got with the Government Life Insurance Office selling acres of land on which they'd grow little trees. And my word he did well. People weren't looking on the dark side. They seemed to be living for today so to speak, and they were quite keen on buying things, bonds, and then my husband was transferred to Blenheim, which was a Cinderella. Our travels started then although he did fairly well, quite well at first.

By then the Depression had loomed up although it wasn't at its height of course. Anyhow, we did have lean times. We knew what it was to go to bed at night the same way we got up in the morning—with empty stomachs. We knew what hunger was. We were going out in the country and coming in contact with all these farmers because of course New Zealand was one big farm. Marlborough was very hard hit because it had no secondary industry.Nelson didn't feel the pinch quite like Blenheim because of secondary industry—food-growing, hops, tomatoes and so on, and so they didn't feel it so badly. Well, we went out and were hearing these tales of woe from the farmers. The first thing that some of them would do would be to ask "Do you want a cow, or do you want a sheep?" They couldn't give them away, and there were too many for them to eat themselves so they were killing them and burying them.

Well, we went along out in the country. I think it was round Hillsden way and my husband pulled up at this place—it was very dilapidated looking, fences down, just hanging—the door was partly open and he said to me "I'm going in there and I don't know what for—something's urging me to go. I don't expect any business. By the look of the farmer here he's in a pretty bad state. But I'm going to have a talk to him." So he went and knocked on the door and there was no reply. He knocked several times and was about to turn away when an elderly man came down the passage. And so my husband introduced himself and said he was representing the Government Life Insurance Office. "Oh," he said, "I can't do anything for the insurances. I haven't a penny to bless myself with. As a matter of fact I'm going off my farm next weekend" And my husband said to him "Are you?" and he said "Yes, I'm getting put off my farm. I'm not making my overheads, I'm in a very poor state." So my husband said "Well, perhaps I could help you." "You could help me? How?" "Well, first of all, have you a policy?"Have you had insurance?" And he said "Yes . . . I have a policy somewhere, but I wouldn't know where, I haven't seen it for years. I don't know where it is." My husband said "Well that's a pity but never mind, you comb the house through and find it because that policy might be your saviour." "Oh," he said, "after all these years?" "It could be. I'm not going to build you up false hopes, but see how long you've let it lie. It may not have lapsed you see." So of course, he said, "I'll come back in a day or two—a few

Many marginally economic farms were kept going only by the virtual slave labour of the farmer's wife and children. A young boy, clad in cavalry breeches, awaits the arrival of the cream lorry to take the daily output to the butter factory. Photo Auckland Weekly News.

days, before the end of the week and give you time to search for it." We went back towards the weekend and he'd found the policy. So my husband looked at it and he said "Well, you're saved. You'll not be going off your farm." "Won't I? Won't it have lapsed after all these years?" And my husband said "No" and pointed out to him the fact that after the policy being in force about two years it would keep going itself for another 2½ years, without paying any premiums. And so he said "Well you're not going off your farm. You take this in to your banker. It's a gilt-edged security. The banker will tide you through." And that really pleased him. So he said "I hope you mean it Mr Hastie." "I wouldn't say it if I didn't mean it." And so he said "I'll come back and see you—not to talk insurance, you can't do anything about that by insuring. I just want to see how you've got along with the banker."

So we went back again and you know the old farmer was a different man altogether. He was just beaming. And he put his hand out and shook my husband's hand and he said "You were a godsend Mr Hastie. You know, that morning you came to me I didn't answer the door straight away. I was in tears. I was down on my knees praying when you came. How strange it is. When I got up off my knees you were standing at the door. There was my saviour at the door." He was very, very thrilled.

There was a scheme called the 'Over the Fence' scheme where farmers were given a few shillings a week to look after a member of unemployed. 'Over the fence' meant that he would be over the fence from off the road and this is why it got that name. Well, farmers just dismissed any staff they had (they couldn't very well afford to keep them anyway) and then hired them back again at unemployment rates instead of standard rates of pay and they had them on their farms as relief workers. Now this is a dreadful situation to pertain in any society. Imagine the strain of an employer/employee relationship which

Reafforestation camp Wanganui September 1933. Unemployed boys planted marram grass on 900 acres of sand dunes for three shillings a week and a share in the enterprise. No-one ever returned to claim their share of mature marram grass. Photo Auckland Weekly News.

had been reasonable, I suppose, when the man was working for the farmer, and then became quite unreasonable when the man had been put into the relief situation. First of all, he was made unemployed and then only employed for a couple of days or three days a week instead of a full week. These things exacerbated social relationships and social ill-feeling for years and years ahead and the farmers in this country were regarded as pretty flinty kind of characters when some of us knew very well that the farmers themselves were in desperate straits and it was very well known that half the dairy farmers in the country were by 1932-33 insolvent and the question arose whether they should be thrown off their farms by the stock and station firms and the banks, or kept on. Well, there was no point in the stock and station firms throwing them off their farms because if the farms were going to yield anything at all they had to have somebody to do the work, so they kept the farmers on the farms but said every penny that comes in from your produce we are going to supervise the expenditure of and so we'll put you on a budget. Budgetting became very dominant as the method of handling the finances of the farmers of New Zealand. Now when you're on a budget and every month the farm manager or the stock and station manager would go over your list of expenditure and say "Look, you're going to spend two pounds this month on your family needs. You can't. Your production is only sufficient for you to spend 30/-. You've got to cut it down." And they'd say "For instance, look, you've got some underclothing for your wife, well can't you cut that out?" Now this is where it got down to discussing individual pieces of clothing, whether the budget would or would not allow it. And usually it had to be cut out, because either you were insolvent and you walked off your farm, or you accepted the budget and worked on your farm. So that for years, particularly the womenfolk and the children, went short not only of food but of clothes and of course any things like travel or any kind of a luxury like buying a bicycle for the youngster. All this sort of thing was completely out. Or getting the water supply from outside the house to inside—that kind of thing would be out because the budget couldn't run to that. The idea was so to supervise the farmer that he could keep on producing for the man to whom he was in debt. So the banker or the stock and station agent got some money towards the repayment of the interest or the payment of debt. But the mortgage relief legislation that came later helped stop this and people who were put on budgets were put on a budget related to the productivity of the farm. But this didn't take place until the end of the Depression. In the beginning of the Depression it was how I've described it.

I remember my father telling me that he'd been "requested" (requested—that's a good one) to hand over his life insurance policy to his banker. I've still got the letter. We'd been farmers in Canterbury since 1851, and we had an overdraft on the stock—4,000 sheep, 56 run cows—of two thousand pounds. We asked a local stock firm to take over the current account, which they did without any demands for the life insurance policy.

Just the other day an acquaintance showed me the farm they owned at Oxford and because they were ninety pounds short on the mortgage the firm they were in debt to closed the account and they were thrown off the property. The manager of that firm later committed suicide by hanging himself. Also, I remember I'd given a neighbour of mine a dog which had won a lot of trophies, and a beautiful kennel to go with it. He was a man who'd been badly knocked about in the first world war—gassed, shrapnell wounds—and he and his wife asked me to take the dog and the kennel back because that same stock firm manager was closing the account and he didn't want them to be just auctioned off. I broke down when I heard that and I sent the local secretary of the RSA ten pounds towards expenses in getting the man made secure on his farm, which was a rehab. farm which he kept very well. The RSA did what they could and the man kept his farm. His son has it now, a very prosperous and well-kept farm.

There was a neighbouring farmer too who told us that he had to present his store account to his firm who used to question him about various items. He remembers once there were two toothbrushes on the account and the manager queried what they were for. "Oh, one for myself and one for my wife," he replied.

"Can't you made do with one?" the manager wanted to know.

I suppose that it was petty humiliation at that level which was what the Depression was all about.

M*y father and Mr Norman Williams were going to go into pigs together. Norman Williams at the time was MP for Kaiapoi and a grain and produce merchant. Well my father had built a very elaborate pigsty for those days . . . it had a loading shed, a huge trough for mixing the pigs' things, very good sleeping quarters for the pigs, a clear place where they could run afterwards, and a central ditch where you swept down the washings from the pig run. And it was all kept completely clean and sweet-smelling. I mean you could go in your best suit into the pig run. My father built that in 1927-28, he built it himself, designed it himself, and it was really excellent. Well they bought pigs—I don't know how much was paid for them in those days—and we had mostly Tamworths and he was feeding them on grain and as a matter of fact his bacon and ham was sought after over most of New Zealand.*

Then Mr Williams went home to England to see what the market was like and while he was there the Depression burst and he cabled home to my father and he said "Sell out of pigs, they're 2½d on the hoof at Smithfield". That was pretty bad, even translated into the prevailing prices at the time, the economy of the time. So my father did sell out. He was lucky that he did, even though most of the pig farmers round about who had the ordinary little sty used to go round the hotels in those days to get great big barrels of swill from the hotels, but even then, that didn't pay the men to grow pigs. Bacon and things went right down. That was the time I remember when butter went down to 11½d a pound.

Well my father was growing onions at the time. Round about August or September the average farmer couldn't sell his onions because they were importing Victorian onions into the Christchurch market. My father grew two crops and he had to carry the onions out again as manure. He just couldn't sell them. So the next year my father sent two bags up COD to Mr Williams and said "Try what you can do with these." Mr Williams took one of the bags into parliament buildings and he offered them for sale and he was swamped. And at that time he and my father had already got together and he was trying to push through a Bill to exclude the Victorian onions for sale against our own onions, and that was one of the ways in which he got the ban on the Victorian onions. The onion market then went right down to zero but my mother had one idea of "saving our bacon" to a certain extent. Her idea was that instead of selling all the big onions to the market, she asked our grocer when he was selling onions in his shop, what he would like to sell. So he said "Well actually housewives don't want all big onions because once they cut into a big onion then it's done, and if they only want a certain amount of onion then they would rather have a few small ones." So mother took him down to the onion shed where she was working and she said: "Now pick me out a sample of the kind of onion that you would like to sell in your shop." Well, he looked through the different grades of onions and picked out what he thought. So mother said

"Well thank you, now there's a sample for your shop, I'll hang on to it as a guide." Which she did. And so instead of putting up large amounts of big onions and then small onions and then big ones in a bag, she got my father to put up samples and she labelled them grocer samples and she found that in the auction rooms they sold very well. That was just a case where initiative paid off, in asking the grocer just exactly what he wanted.

Well, as you can guess, when you had your land on a mortgage (and we were paying 8½% at the time on the mortgage and the man wanted his money out), we were going to go to the wall. The house was mortgaged in order to buy that land. Several farmers who had mortgages on their land—round about here anyway—just simply walked off their land. Their land was repossessed. And my father was going to be in that position, then the government moratorium came into force and of course he had to go to the court and to display all his receipts and returns for about four years before. And he was granted a moratorium, which meant they couldn't be turned out of their property, and also in that time I think, interest went down from 8% to 4½% which made quite a difference to us. Instead of having to pay about ninety-five pounds a year, we had to pay about forty-five pounds a year . . . at least it made very nearly that difference. Well you can guess that made quite a difference when they had to be paid twice yearly because in May and November it was always a terrific struggle to get our interest.

Everybody was in the same boat. I mean . . . the men . . . it was really tragic to see them going around from door to door. They were trying to sell notepaper and bits and pieces and things to try and earn a crust really. And it was very tragic . . . we didn't have any money to buy this stuff and mother very often would put up some sandwiches and give them a cup of tea and put up a bottle of tea for them, she was so sorry for them. Some of them looked so down-hearted when they left the place. And of course behind these hedges, you see, people sort of expect a large house and they still expected the farmers to have the money to be able to buy.

Right from our early childhood there never seemed to be enough of anything, and the Depression days were much the same only worse. I married in March 1929 at a time when my husband was a shepherd on the Cascade Station near Culverdon at three pounds a week and found in the basics only—flour, sugar, bread, milk, butter and eggs. Our first son was born in May 1931, wool prices dropped just after that and we were given a week's notice and left with about fifty pounds (a lot of money then) owing in wages. The boss had thirteen race horses and he and his sons did very little work on the station. We would have had to use up all our savings before we could get relief so we put every thing into a ten acre block at Waimate. There was no electricity and water was drawn by a windlass from a 43-feet deep well. The mortgage payments were at 7% and we practically lived off the farm. We had our own butter, milk and eggs and we sold surplus eggs to buy groceries. Sausages were eighteen for a shilling, salad bananas were 24 for a shilling, and knitting wool sixteen shillings a pound so our children had mostly knitted clothing.

Over the years four children were born and I went into the nursing home perched up in a gig pulled by a half draught horse. We bought our first second-hand cot for half-a-crown. It wasn't until 1938 that we could buy a car, an old Whippet, for seventy-five pounds. We gradually added to the farm, a ten-acre block here, a few acres there. An electrician friend wired up our old wooden cottage for five pounds and sold us an old Pacific radio, a real monster. I think I got my first electric iron for a bucket of strawberries and a bucket of rasp-berries. We often bartered goods and services with our neighbours. We used to borrow records and have a party although there was never any alcohol—nobody could afford it.

I can remember a few recipes too. To make a milkshake we used to beat an egg yolk with milk and a little bit of sugar and flavouring, add a cup of milk and lastly a beaten egg white. The kids loved them and they were extremely nourishing. All our sweets were homemade, or we used to buy raisins at eightpence a packet. Fizzy drinks we made out of home-made fruit salts. A quarter of a pound of tartaric acid, a quarter of baking soda, the same of Epsom salts, icing sugar and cream of tartar, and one ounce of magnesia. We used to keep it well corked and add a teaspoonful to a glass of water. Banana jelly and cream was a treat to our family because we kept just the bare minimum of cream and made the rest into butter which we sold at eightpence a pound. So a few years ago when my grandchildren were staying I promised them a very nice pudding. You should have seen their faces when they were confronted with it. "Gee," they said, "ole banana jelly."

And there's one thing that's always stuck in my mind. A friend of mine worked at Woollies. One Friday night a girl bought a roll of toilet paper and on Monday wanted to return it. My friend asked why and the girl replied:"The visitors didn't come." Newspaper was the order of the day then.

In my opinion, for very many farmers, the Depression would be a heightening of an existing situation. Sometimes it would be fairly drastic, but at the same time at the time of the Depression there were a great many farmers who were struggling to keep on their land and the effect of the Depression would be that a considerable number were unable to remain there.

The situation of the farmers in the 1920s before the Depression was a varied one. They had of course a very big burst of prosperity during the war when wool particularly was selling tremendously well. After that the period of prosperity went on I think for two or three years after the war till about 1923 when world markets were considerably affected and many of the farmers were in trouble. From 1929 on, those men who had been desperately endeavouring to maintain their hold on their farms would be very gravely affected by the general effects of the Depression.

It was first of all the question of markets. The markets went to pieces to some extent, but then of course the necessary things that they wanted for instance say manures, wire, all that kind of business, very often went up tremendously in price or alternatively were not even on supply. It would really mean this: that every member of the family would have to work and work extremely hard, wife and children in the sheds and all that kind of business, and at the end, not even able to make the farm pay, they'd have to get off.

I was at Wesley College during those days and the effect upon the college was considerable. Our roll was almost cut in half for a time, we had to put teachers off, salaries went down to some extent and it was a desperate struggle to keep the school going, because most of our full fee-paying boys came from a farming community, and of course farms were all affected by the Depression.

Probably a fair percentage of the boys who were established at the school, their parents would make a desperate attempt to keep them going and a fairly high percentage probably were kept going. But where we really lost was on the boys who never came at all. So that suddenly one day there weren't so many boys. The enrolments just went down like that. You wouldn't be able to measure it in specific terms, that is that such and such a boy didn't come; all you knew was that your enrolment wasn't what it would've been. Of course we also lost boys who were on our roll but who couldn't come back say for a further year, something of that sort. Their parents just couldn't make it.

And of course back of that, there was a good deal of frustration and upset. The whole school was operating almost on a poverty level, for instance school supplies, all that sort of thing. During the Depression this was true not only of private schools like Wesley College, but it'd be true also of the national schools that the general supply of equipment and so forth to schools was heavily cut. And this had a bad effect. The teacher in the classroom operated with slightly less equipment. There was a bit of a cut all over, but on the whole there was an enormous cut over the country. But in any school, supplies—and sometimes supplies had a very vital part to play in it—would be very considerably cut. For instance there was no abundance of extra readers or anything of that sort. That kind of thing went by the board.

In 1929 I'd been in New Zealand about nine years. I'd come out here to marry a New Zealand farmer, a returned soldier. He took me to an isolated backblocks farm, miles from anywhere or anyone. It was in Northland, or North Auckland as the province was then called. Those first nine years were terrible enough, but when the second, for us, Depression began in 1929 things became desperate. My husband had a farm under the returned soldiers' scheme and the government took a lien on everything very promptly. We had two children by this time and we'd only just managed to get a car the year before. This was laid up in the garage and on rare trips to get stores we used a horse and buggy. 'Stores' is a euphemism, I only bought flour, sugar, baking powder and tea, and I recall monthly accounts at the one local store eight miles away being two pounds or less. We could eat well fortunately because we had our own mutton, a vegetable garden, ample fruit for preserving and jam, and of course milk and eggs. I made butter and I'd always made our own bread right from the beginning, as soon as I knew how. I even made the children's slippers myself, with several thicknesses of sugarbag topped with any old woollen material for soles, and whatever could be cut up from old outdoor clothes for the uppers. I taught the children myself through the Correspondence School, and I can't speak too highly of them.

I recall one memorable day when the bill for the insurance premium arrived and my husband and I counted the *only* cash we had, kept in a tobacco tin, to see if there was sufficient to meet the account and luckily there was. He sent away twelve sheepskins on one occasion with about three inches of wool on them, and received in payment ten penny stamps!

In 1932 I was seriously ill and I had to go to Auckland for an operation. I went to see the then Commissioner of Crown Lands,off my own bat, to tell him how we'd literally slaved for twelve years and were disheartened. He told me they could take all the furniture—even household belongings—such as they were. That was the last straw and I replied that I'd burn them first. I'm not an aggressive type, in fact I'd been brought up gently in England, but enough is enough. My temerity paid off. While I was away he himself went up to our farm with the local officials, saw and heard how we worked and so on, and there was a happy result. We were given a really terrific revaluation, orders given that the house which was huge, leaking, and with no conveniences, should be fixed, and from then on we went ahead, so that we were able to sell out twenty years ago and buy our present farm only nine miles from the city.

I wouldn't want anyone to experience what we did during those years, though I do believe that as a result parents tried too hard to save their families from such hardships with the result that the youngsters now want everything laid on. Those years were a challenge to be overcome and looking back I wonder that such poverty and hardship were to be borne, although it was made easier by knowing that everyone was in the same boat.

Women And Children First

My man's gone now. He had to go.
He couldn't find no work around this town.
Not for ages. Used his wages.
Got up this morning—and he was gone.

Monday morning. It starts to rain.
Around the curve there comes a south-bound train.
Under a tarpaulin rides a bum called John.
He was a strange man, but he is gone.

Morning sunshine. The rooster crows.
Along the highway walking to where, goodness knows.
Where's John sleeping? How's he keeping?
When will he take the homeward road?

My man's gone now. He had to go.
He couldn't find no work around this town.
Not for ages. Used his wages.
Got up this morning—and he was gone.

To me the Depression isn't something I can easily put my finger on and say, oh, such and such happened on such and such an occasion, it's more a whole awful experience, the terrible, terrible feeling of dread at school when you were told you had to get another book, exercise or text, it didn't matter and you dragged your feet all the way home. Awful at the beginning of the school year too: they must have been very small lists because it was a primary school but they always sent my father demented and we always knew they would. I have thought since that my parents, who were married very young and who had done what in England is called 'skipped a class' were terribly insecure financially —both determined to 'have' or 'make' a good home and all that, and how things looked mattered. They were also very young when we were born and I think allowed us to know how worried stiff they were about money when we were far too young to cope with that sort of worry. I mean, if they'd just said: "Well, there isn't a lot of money but we'll get there *somehow*", but they never thought of that last phrase. I know I often felt, aged about nine I suppose, almost responsible for the family finances.

I now know that my father had just got his first branch in the bank, the youngest manager they'd appointed. But no sooner had he got it than they had a ten per cent salary cut, followed by another, so I guess they were feeling very knocked back indeed. Oh, and the rent went up. All the same I wish they hadn't bothered with *furniture*—people wouldn't bother today—oh, I suppose some would.

One specific memory: we arrived in Auckland—I went with mother to the estate agent's to find a house. She listed her needs: three bedrooms, separate dining room, walking distance of school and bank (to save bus fares), decent-sized garden, and we went and looked at five places which met all these requirements and ended up in Remuera Road among the high-life pouffeys, paying heaven knows what tiny rent by today's standards.

Photo NZ Herald.

We were badly burgled too when we were away at a (borrowed) beach house at Titirangi—clothes, records, playing cards, as well as the usual stuff. They found a lot of it in second-hand dealers in Karangahape Road and mother and dad had to buy it back. The police explained that if they just took it the dealers would never co-operate with them again. Besides the cost there was also the gall; they even bought back some of their own wedding presents, silver and stuff. The police did catch the burglars. But mostly there was this awful sense of absolute catastrophe if any unexpected expenditure was suddenly thrust upon us.

When you're a child you don't notice things like Depressions very much, especially if your family is quite well off—as mine was. I heard my mother and father talking about it of course, but it was just a word. But I do remember one thing which just stuck out as an oddity at the time but which, looking back, was obviously a Depression sort of thing. There were two twin boys in my class and some days one would be barefoot and sometimes the other, and after a while I realised that they only had one pair of shoes between them, so I suppose it was a case of first up best dressed. A lot of children never had any shoes at all, mind you, and it was taken very much for granted.

It wasn't until years afterwards that I knew there had been a Depression, but it was a peculiar time, a time of strange happenings. My father hardly ever being home, my mother worried, and my sister and I escorted to and from school for a while when the unrest grew to riot proportions. It was a time of excitement, Ted the police undercover man arriving at odd times, slipping in through the wash-house to report "party activities" to my father, and sometimes staying to babysit while mother and father had a rare outing together. We loved this. Ted had been a school teacher in Australia and we never tired of his stories or his company. He came under suspicion finally and had to be shipped to Australia rather hurriedly. I remember in the beginning he had made the mistake of wearing old worn clothes and then, because none of the Communist Party had any money, he had to continue wearing them so as not to arouse suspicion. His chance came with the riots and looting. He put in an appearance wearing new shoes and a new shirt. "Look at old Ted!" someone said. "He's a sly one. Look at those shoes and that shirt."

It was a time of change. At school Bernice and I had sat together since the primers, but in standard two we along with several others were separated. My new desk companion Mae was a tall shambling girl with a wide wet grin and long bare chilblained cold-looking feet. I can only ever remember her wearing one frock, cotton with white and blue flowers on an orange background. She wore it with an apron for a week, then without an apron for a week, and then she didn't come to school at all for a day or two days, and no one asked for a note. It was the same with some of the others.

At lunch time we didn't go out when the bell rang. We had 20 minutes for lunch at our desks before we went to play. We had to open up our lunches and our teacher went round dividing them up and giving a share to each girl who had no lunch to eat—in fact some children often didn't even have breakfast.

I used to take a cut lunch every day except Friday (three-pence of fish and chips and three plain cakes or two cream cakes), and I remember very distinctly watching my mother wrap my lunch one morning and putting in a beautiful little miniature jam roll. All morning I thought about that roll, looking forward to the moment when I would take it out and eat it, savouring every crumb.

That moment never came.

The teacher carefully dividing the lunches between the haves and the have-nots pushed the chocolate lamington to my side and the beautiful little jam roll to Mae's. I can still feel the horror, and wonder why I didn't say something. But I didn't. Teachers' decisions were not questioned in those days. I watched Mae eat two peanut butter sandwiches and then my jam roll. I watched her as she sat smiling her wide wet smile, her mouth outlined in white icing sugar, and somehow whenever anyone mentions the "Depression", to me it all seems wrapped up in that one incident, all centred in a jam roll.

If my father was typical, I think there was a great deal of shame in the minds of working men who found themselves on relief work, who had to go with an order from the Charitable Aid Board for groceries up to the local Self Help. If I remember rightly, my parents used to spell out C.A.B. so that I wouldn't know what it meant and of course kids always know a hell of a lot more than their parents think, and I knew that we were going up with a C.A.B. chit to get groceries and what this meant. I think one of the lessons that I took out of that—even at that early age—was that if it ever came to a similar situation again, I'd be annoyed, I might do all sorts of things, but I'd never be ashamed because it gave me an attitude—you know—bugger them, whereas I'm afraid my poor father was badly affected by it. He took to the booze as many of his contemporaries did with whatever money they could get. Sometimes he took a loan out on our furniture unbeknown to anybody else in the family until such time as some debt collecting agency came around.

The C.A.B. chits were for groceries. I can remember I used to have Creamota that came from there. They were in fact for people who were unable to feed their families on the money that was given out. I was an only child so that we were a small family and, by and large, there's no question that we were quite reasonably if not over well-fed during the Depression. I think I probably had bad dietary habits as a child—far too much fishcakes and fish and chips and not enough good food, but certainly no question of starving. This was because of the size of the family. Opposite us there were two or three families where there was real neglect and real trouble and two or three of the mothers went into mental hospitals. I suppose Dad could get away from the place and go and get boozed if he could get the money but it was the mums that obviously broke down under the strain of seeing large families they knew they couldn't care for. They became completely hopeless and broke down.

Some of the kids of course shoplifted, but then some kids do that today—but they were doing it from necessity rather than from kicks. There were instances in which people were absolutely forced to do something which was outside of the law. One of the cases I remember was of a friend of my mother's who was deserted by her husband while pregnant—she had a couple of other kids as well. She had hardly any money at all to live on and with the baby coming went to the local church jumble sale (which of course was for charity but she was one of the sort of people that were supposed to be helped). She was told that she had to pay for things and of course she had just nothing to pay with. So she and my mother—who had a number of very good qualities including obviously of getting away with things from the jumble sale—outfitted the baby very well by shoplifting the charity goods which had been donated by people to the church for charitable purposes. So I suppose they were carrying out the wishes of the original donor by ensuring that there was no money taken from the poor for things that they absolutely needed. This of course was before the days of social security and maternity benefit.

This same woman went into labour at her home and wanted a doctor. Well, there was no question of going to a hospital in her mind, she thought she'd have it at home. The first doctor approached was a man who had better remain nameless, but who was later the Chairman of the Auckland branch of the British

Relief Workers Cheaper THAN HORSES!

" So far as men engaged on Roadwork are concerned, the ideal " must be to move them ' over the fence ' on to the land."

THUS spoke the Rt. Hon. J. G. Coates, who with the Rt. Hon. G. Forbes is joint leader of the Government in Parliament. The above photograph is of relief workers working under his department, and shows what he means.

Women of New Zealand!

WILL YOU STAND FOR THIS?

This Government professes to save your country, but reduces your sons, your husbands, your brothers to the cheapness of horses. It is in YOUR power to effect a change in Government by voting **LABOUR** and let New Zealand be once again *" God's own Country."*

'This !–In God's Own Country !' The Shade of R. J. Seddon watches relief workers dragging a chain harrow. The highlight of Labour's propaganda in the 1931 election campaign

Labour Party advertisement 1931. It took four years of this for the electorate to share Seddon's views and sweep Labour to power in 1935. Photo Alexander Turnbull Library.

Medical Association, and he wanted to know if she could pay before he would come. This telephoning was done by my father, not by her, she was in labour at this stage. After a consultation with other people in the street, he was advised to go to another doctor . . . as far as the first one was concerned of course anything could have happened and if the money wasn't there he didn't care. The second man, who didn't rise to eminence in his profession, and was in some ways a fairly narrow Christian in temperance, non-drinking and so on . . . he was well-known for the fact that he put a number of the principles he happened to believe into practice. You only had to ring him and he would come; any question of money would be secondary. This also happened when I was sick, he attended me several times then and in later years—he was our doctor for quite some time. But it was interesting to see just what problems were faced by the poor.

We had a shilling in the slot gas meter and if you didn't have a shilling and hoped you would have by the time the gas-man came, the art was to cut a circular piece of cardboard so that the shilling would be registered. Of course it was inevitable that the gas-man would come sometimes, like the iceman, and that he would want to know the story. But a lot of these officials—except when there was a new one on the route who wouldn't know what the story was—were pretty reasonable people and provided they were protected and that there was a shilling there when they came around, they were OK. There was talk that one fellow didn't worry too much about the shillings and used to collect from the ladies in other ways, but this is only talk I overheard later on and I didn't have any first-hand experiences.

I went to a school just down the street and kids were mostly like us, and when I went later to Beresford Street school which was just around the road too, the children were all from working class families. I spent a short time at the Catholic school, where I think perhaps I got one of my best early lessons on the connection between social class and religion. The particular priest was not a very good teacher in the modern sense; he lined everybody up who'd made a mistake in their long division and would hit them with a stick if they had not found their mistake by the time he got to them in the queue. Of course this induced mental paralysis when you thought you were going to be really walloped. However, he never did this to the son of the publican who gave fifty pounds to the church at Easter. And this is where, in that context, we became aware of a difference between us and the others. We were aware of local differences.

Now there was one man who would nowadays be regarded as a very common or garden working man, it's so funny now even to think about it. This poor gentleman was actually a lowly railway worker and having no children was paying off his house on mortgage. The rest of us were all on rent, when we could pay the rent, and the railway worker was regarded as a kind of obscenity in the neighbourhood, a kind of member of the oppressing classes. One of our less delicate kids did a shit in a great big piece of paper one day and threw it over into his yard for the express purpose of expressing the disgust that they had of this house owner.

You could buy loaves that were returned to the bakery, yesterday's bread. You could go down and get broken biscuits fairly cheaply from Bycrofts factory. The problem as I experienced it as a child wasn't very bad because we had such a small family and the cost of sausages at 4d a pound and mince at 6d a pound—although it had to be related to how much money you had in your pocket—was such that I was never conscious of going without food, nor my parents going without food. I think it was possibly their own attitudes as well as just the lack of money that resulted in a not very good diet. We always seemed to have a halfpenny for a chew bar, or something like that . . . that was ourselves. Mind you, other kids just didn't have any money at all.

We were all asked at the Catholic school to bring down some money for a certain priest's presentation. Only those who brought money down were allowed to go to the Winter Show, which was free for all school children. So in other words the school was imposing a bar on those kids who weren't putting money into this guy's presentation. I remember my mother, after saying some words that I hadn't heard before and relating them to the Catholic church in general gave this kid over the road threepence and so he went. There were people around the place who didn't have any money at all.

I'd have been four years old in 1929 and we were living in Nelson, just starting to feel the effects of hardship at that time. My father and my mother's brother set off to cycle down to Christchurch and we had enough money—as I found out later—for mother and I to go by service car. We got down by Cheviot and a couple of trampish-looking people on the side of the road hailing the service car actually turned out to be my father and my mother's brother. They sat at the back of the old service car; my mother didn't want to be associated with "those people" at that stage. But thinking back it sort of struck me that they weren't very well-looking people and I could understand in a few years after that why we didn't recognise them.

There were odd jobs going in Christchurch at that stage and later on when the Depression really hit, of course, there was no work at all. I recall that my father refused to go on the dole and would take anything that was going, one of the jobs being to work in a gravel pit, a thing he'd never done in his life before. He got into this gravel pit which was some ten miles away and he used to bike to work. The first morning he biked to work and that night he wheeled the bike home because he was too stiff and sore to ride, in fact his hands were completely blistered. I well remember my mother saying "Well, you're not going back there again because you can get the same money for going on the dole." But dad was one of those stubborn pig-headed people who believed that there was more self-respect in working, so he went back the next morning.

Dad was very bitter because of the lack of opportunity for work for himself and lack of money to give the things to mother and myself that he wanted to give. My mother was more sorrowful of the fact that there was just not enough food to live on properly and that by the time we paid the rent there was virtually nothing left to live on from the money coming into the house.

I don't think it really struck me as a child that I should feel badly, it's only in later years that I've sort of thought back on it and found that the results of inequalities . . . there was a certain amount of resentment of those kids who seemed to have everything, who could afford fish and chips for their lunch or bought an apple or an orange, whereas we had bread and dripping. And on very very special occasions we'd get some jam or something like this. Never had meat sandwiches and things like that.

I can well remember lying in my bedroom, next to the kitchen, and hearing mother saying "We've got an egg and I've cooked it for your breakfast", and my father turning round and saying "No, I don't feel hungry this morning, give it to the boy." It wasn't until afterwards that I realised that this was the only egg we had in the place. This was the way things were going. Possibly the most noticeable effect of it was one Christmas—the first time I officially knew that there was no Father Christmas. My mother broke the news to me because all the presents they had for us, or for me, was a cheap colouring book and a packet of crayons to the total value I think of 6d from Woolworths. She told me that this was all they could afford and that was it. I went out on Christmas morning—we were living in St Albans at that stage, in a furnished house for which we paid 10/- a week—and there were other boys there. They had bikes and trucks and all sorts of toys and being a little bit full of pride I can remember saying "I've got lots of things but I'm not allowed to bring them out to play with", rather than admit that all we had for my Christmas was a colouring book and crayons.

I'd be about six when I first saw bread queues. I was walking along with my mother and I saw this long queue of people and I asked her what it was and she said it was people queueing up to get their free issue of bread. The queue actually went round about three sides of a block in Christchurch and I asked her why we didn't get our bread that way and was told that since dad was working we were able to buy a loaf of bread and that these were for people who were on the dole and didn't have any money so they got the free loaf issue of bread. It seemed to me funny that some people had to stand for hours in a queue and others, ourselves included could go along to a shop and buy a loaf of bread. But the thing that in retrospect strikes me most about this queue was the sort of patience . . . that people stood in line patiently shuffling forward a little bit at a time. I watched it for a while on several occasions because my mother had shopping to do or people to see, and I used to stand and watch them. Thinking back on it I can see the sort of patience . . . almost servility, of people standing there shuffling forward a little bit at a time to get their loaf of bread.

I think one of the things that I've remembered from childhood during the Depression is the big truck that used to come out from town. The furniture truck. I still can't think of it without a shiver, it seemed so ominous. It was the truck that used to come and take away the furniture of people who were in debt and who had a summons taken out against them. I can remember clinging to my mother and asking: "They won't take our furniture away, will they mum?"

The sort of way that the Depression struck us most forcibly as kids was first of all, the family situation, as my mother was widowed. My father died a couple of months before I was born and she was living on a widow's pension, which was very inadequate. There was a general feeling of poverty. Perhaps it was artificially induced in a way, because my mother's standard of living had collapsed because my father had a relatively high salary as an engineer. She felt it very much, having to scrape and stint and we didn't wear shoes.

We were living near Khandallah, and one felt because of family background a sense of identity with the well-to-do. There was another branch of humanity at the school—the camp kids. There was a public works camp for relief workers just off Onslow Road, and these kids had a much greater distance to walk to school, because the school was on the old side of Khandallah. The other side of Khandallah was always referred to as "the other side". This was the new part, where state houses were built in due course, but there were odd houses scattered around, mostly cheaper houses, smaller houses. The kids that came from the camp were definitely another breed altogether, or so they were regarded. I think the main bulk of the camp workers at the time were being used for road works of some sort or another, in Wellington. I think they were shipped by truck to the place where the actual job was; Anderson Park was being built, the park at the top of Wellington College grounds was being built, the top of Mount Victoria was being levelled. There was a steady supply of labour from this source.

We always regarded the camp kids as something quite separate and apart from us even though I used to look uneasily at my feet and was in fact in the exact situation as they were. The odd thing is, you meet these kids now, kids who are now older men like me, and they are actually marvellous human beings, who have grown up with all sorts of deprivations and so on and yet have survived and for the most part are very interesting people. They've got various chips on their shoulders, some of them, but very good people to have a beer with and a yarn to. I think we all probably benefitted by this sort of inter-mixture that went on at school. That's one thing. Another thing is—there was a large number of people wandering around the streets selling things. Mainly the people who had collapsed in their life-style due to the slump, obviously, as we look at it now. And I would imagine small businessmen, shopkeepers, people of this sort who lost everything and who wanted to maintain their independence and their gentility. They often had a very good line of patter, usually selling soap or combs, something everybody probably needed and they could easily persuade people selling from door to door. My mother had a feeling that they were some sort of drones, parasites, and she would chase them off the premises. I think this was the general feeling of a lot of people, that these people had no right to be coming around, and yet they kept coming. I take it they made a living somehow—they must have found a soft touch at one door or another.

Another thing was the road works themselves. I remember actually seeing some of the jobs being done unnecessarily. There were a couple of corners up on the Ngaio Gorge, where men with picks worked away for two or three winters in succession. During summer they were taken away and used on some other job, but during the winter you'd see these blokes working through rain or shine. This was the main route from Khandallah to town. The old Bell Bus Service operated, and as a child I saw quite a lot of these blokes at work. I remember the faces—the kind of faces that a child remembers—tough, rough faces.

This doesn't seem to have much to do with the Depression, but in fact it has, because you identified a kind of face. Maybe this is a literary way of looking at life but I remember it was about this same time (might have been a bit earlier), waking up to go to the dental clinic in town with my mother and older brother and sister. I think perhaps they'd been to the dental clinic and I hadn't and I was somehow able to associate the day with that smell, with the dental clinic's waiting room and comics. However, it was a general outing and we always went afterwards to Adams Bruce and had an ice-cream, which was a real treat. But waiting for the bus, it must have been midafternoon or it might have been mid-morning, I can't quite recall the time of day, I remember seeing a march which my mother told me was the unemployed. There was this endless, endless stream of people marching along the end of Lambton Quay into parliament grounds, and these were all the same sort of faces which we thought of—the heavily lined faces, like faces that had been in the open air a lot. I had uncles who were farmers who had faces that were similar, although they were better fed than these ones. These ones were gaunt; not so fussy about shaving. It was the cheerfulness of them too, that although there was something threatening and menacing to a small boy with a large crowd of males, there was a sort of cheerfulness about them, there were banners and they were singing. I can't remember what they were singing. It was the first demonstration I had ever witnessed, and I associated it with the sort of pictures you saw of the French Revolution—this was something really big going on and terribly impressive.

Walter Bromley had been assistant secretary of the Labour Party towards the end of Walter Nash's national secretaryship, but he gave it up to join the Labour Department. He was regarded by the unions and the unemployed as the designer of the relief schemes, and there was acute bitterness particularly when we became the government in 1935 and his services were retained. It was said that he had prepared two relief plans, one for use if the

ɪoto Alexander Turnbull Library.

Tories were returned, and another if Labour were successful, but whether that was true I don't know.

There were over 750 women trapesing the streets of Wellington looking for work. The Mayoress' Relief Committee was providing a mid-day dinner cooked by unemployed women in the old Technical College. It also paid room rents not exceeding seven shillings; and with such rooms, bare and drab, the poor landladies were no better off than the women. The Committee also provided weekend packets of tea, sugar, 2 ounces of butter, and bread. There was also a subsidised scheme for domestic help not exceeding ten shillings. If an employer offered ten shillings, seven and sixpence, five shillings or half a crown a week, the subsidy was the same. Many girls went to homes for nothing if the visiting agent, Mrs Forde, approved of the home. Pat Lenihen and Ivy Snow were both members of the Women's Branch and both unemployed. They brought information of brow-beating when girls rejected jobs offering no remuneration.

I was going into the Trades Hall on the tram one day, when Walter Bromley hopped on at his stop. I immediately tackled him about the women and girls. I told him women were paying three-quarters of a million pounds a year in unemployment tax, and they were getting charity, worse than English poor law relief, and he darned well knew it. He looked me firmly in the eye. "The right kind of woman could change it."

What could we do?

We called a meeting of unemployed women in the Trades Hall to form an association. Alex Croskery and Adam Black, both trades union secretaries, came in to help us draft a constitution. We wanted the women to do it themselves, but most were too miserable even to think. Margaret Semple was elected president and I took the secretaryship. Several good women came forward for executive positions. The Trades and Labour Council gave us a big room, the Gas Company put in two used gas stoves, we fixed up washing and ironing facilities, and every day made one good mid-day meal for nearly a hundred girls. Somebody was in charge all day so that girls had somewhere to come and go.

I made a register and got some press notices. Mrs Knox Gilmer, who was Dick Seddon's daughter, May, gave us seven dozen meat pies every day throughout those awful winters.

It is hard to describe past misery; it's like toothache—when it's gone, it's hard to recall. They say old men forget but old women never forget. The 1934 and 1935 winters were terrible.

We arranged a mass deputation to the prime minister. I insisted that the women should speak for themselves, and we picked out four. Peter Fraser introduced them and those nervous desperate women told their own story. Mr Coates was most impressed.

I was added to the Mayoress' Committee which was composed of representatives of voluntary women's organisations. The Unemployed Bureau For Women in Boulcott Street was also manned by volunteers, a part of the organisation. Five unemployed women and myself waited on two most reactionary women at the Bureau, who had harried girls chiefly in connection with the unpaid jobs. I was armed with statistics that Elizabeth McCombs had compiled: a list of skilled women's names and occupations, together with their unemployment tax contributions over a period of years; and we asked them if other women, married and well off, should offer them employment for no wages at all and brow-beat them when they refused. We said this constituted slavery.

The two women at the Bureau resigned. The first meeting of the Mayoress' Committee that I attended also ended abruptly. Mrs Forde said that women who employed girls in the home expected just as much for half a crown as for ten shillings. I said that I wouldn't stand for making flesh of one and fowl of another, and as for the scheme to train women for domestic work in technical school classes, I knew these women and it would be like teaching one's grandmother to suck eggs. There were skilled women of every kind among them: machine workers, bookbinders, seamstresses, cooks, hotel workers, university students.

I remember one flighty girl who stole a coat and wore it in Willis Street. She was picked up and the police came for me. Only sixteen, she had been in orphanages since she was four, poor child. I went down to the police station and as we walked along Willis Street she told me she was a Roman Catholic, so I turned off into the Presbytery of St Mary's in Boulcott Street. While we were waiting for Father to come, she tried on all the different priests' hats which were lying on a hall seat. When I saw her safely on the train to go to a convent for three months, she said, "Oh heck, I'll only have to pray."

One day I had word of a really good job at the Paekakariki Hotel at seventeen and sixpence a week. I had been watching one sad-faced girl so I left the fare to Paekakariki and a nice little note for her. To my consternation she was at dinner next day. I walked over. "Look dear, if you don't take a job like this you cut the ground from under my feet." She looked sullen and I said, "Come on, take it." She burst into tears. "Mrs Thorn, I'm half engaged to a man and if I go away it will fizzle out and I'll never get another chance."

There was a story going the rounds about a woman and the Public Trust. I don't know how true it was and I couldn't possibly verify it, but here it is for what it's worth. Apparently this woman had been evicted from her house because she couldn't pay the rent. She was a widow, or perhaps her husband had walked out on her, I don't know, but she had three children, one about five, the other two just toddlers. And she went down to the Public Trust office to see if they could rent her a house. Well, they said that they couldn't help her, nothing they could do, she'd have to go and look for somewhere herself.

Well she said: "How can I go looking for a house when I've got three small children and no one to look after them for me?"

"That's your problem, madam," they said.

"Oh is it?" said she, and before they could make a move she was off out the door leaving the three children there for the Public Trust to look after. She didn't actually go house-hunting at all, she just went to visit a friend and have a peaceful afternoon without the children. Around about office closing time back she went to the Public Trust and sure enough, just as she'd thought, they'd found her a house. The thought of having to look after those kids was more than they could stand. She got her house.

In 1929 I was about twelve years old and at primary school. Dad had a job as a machinist for a timber mill. He used to cut willow trees in the Ashley River bed in the spring, and dry them, then he'd cart them home towards the end of summer on a borrowed trailer, then he'd saw them up into fence posts with a home-made saw and stroke engine. We weren't very well off but we used to shoot rabbits, catch trout sometimes, dad used to get wood from work, and we had a glasshouse for growing early vegetables. But in 1930 and 1931 things started to get a bit tough. Dad was reduced to part-time at the saw mill.

By this stage I was at high school at Ashburton Tech. I remember my parents couldn't afford to buy me a school uniform. I used to wear sandshoes instead of the regulation black shoes, and a pale pink blouse of my sister's instead of the white one. We couldn't afford a serge gymslip either so I used to wear navy blue cotton. Then in 1933 I had to leave school. I was sixteen years old and five months pregnant, my husband five years older. We rented a cottage for six shillings a week on half an acre of land near Tinwald, about two and a half miles from my parents' place. It wasn't much of a place. A wood range, bare floors with sacks for mats, no bath, no inside running water. We used to steal farmers' turnips and potatoes and mushrooms to keep alive, and once a week I used to walk the two and a half miles home for a visit and something to eat. My husband had a bit of a job as a contract ploughman, but when I was in the home with our first son he lost his job and went on the dole, twenty-five shillings for three weeks and then a week's stand-down. Dad used to give us fish to keep us going and many's the time I took the pea rifle and went about a mile down the road to the plantation to shoot a rabbit so we'd have something to eat for supper.

I always made our own soap by boiling fat and caustic soda in a kerosene tin over a fire outside. We used to use kerosene tin boxes for furniture. Then my husband borrowed a hundred pounds against an insurance policy I had, to buy himself a truck to cut timber on contract. He had a six-foot crosscut saw and a sledge hammer and wedges and that was all his tools. But it was no good. No one had the money to buy timber for fencing, and he failed. About then we moved to Timaru and took a four-bedroom house at Saltwater Creek for fifteen bob. We went back on the dole, so my husband was away most of the time on dole project work.

What I remember most about that time is hand-outs, grocery orders, meat once a week, usually tough old beef. I used to cut second-hand clothes down for the children. I can remember going to the hospital Charitable Aid Board many times with a sad tale and coming home with orders for groceries and fruit. If you were sick, of course, you didn't go near the doctor, you went to the outpatients department at the public hospital and queued for hours for attention. Luckily I had a treadle sewing machine, and in those days you got family benefit after the first two children, if you qualified under the means test. It was two shillings a week. I furnished the beds for the children from those two shillings. I certainly learned how to feed a family from nothing. I used to keep chooks. Silver beet, mashed spuds and a poached egg was a feast, or sometimes we'd have 'cocky's joy'—fried scones with golden syrup. Apart from one new frock, coat and hat in ten years I made all our clothes out of cast-offs.

It was a great day when grandfather died. I inherited all his underwear and I made a whole lot of warm woollen singlets for the children out of it. Seven kids in ten years. People used to help out a bit. The rabbit factory at Saltwater Creek used to give us bruised rabbits and the Chinese market gardeners would often toss in a few vegetables. My husband and others often stole food from railway waggons and warehouses. He was caught once, but I can't remember the penalty. There were always big bills at the grocer and the butcher which never got paid, but we weren't under too much pressure. It's only from later reading that I've discovered that food was dumped while we starved.

In the end my marriage broke up and I'm sure it was because of the Depression. You can't just go on year after year scraping and scratching without it taking it out on your soul. After a while it just wasn't any use and we agreed to separate. The children were placed in homes and I sallied out into the world again with one pound and my possessions in a suitcase. Even when the Labour Party got in, my husband got work with the Public Works and we thought we'd found a saviour in Michael Savage, it was no good. The Depression had just pushed us too far down to come up. I think that the Depression stole ten years out of my life.

In 1929 we shifted to Christchurch and my husband had a job in a factory at Hornby, but about a year after that the company folded up. No one realised there was a Depression coming and we mortgaged ourselves to the hilt and went into business with a small produce shop. The Depression started to really hit New Zealand about that time and we had no capital to buy stock as trade slackened. We had four children at the time and I had a hard time of it living in the kitchen with no heating and a young baby. I was on my own because Ted took a job shovelling coal for the railway and I had to look after the shop too. People were very kind, the milkman went on supplying milk because he knew we had a baby—he never said a word, and a Plunket nurse arrived one day with a big bag of Weetbix which was very welcome, but we eventually had to sell the shop at a loss and move into a rented house. My husband was out of work and there was a strike of the unemployed when the government tried to cut the relief workers' ration. The children had two meals of just boiled barley and I took my first trip to the relief depot and was granted a loaf of bread, butter, that sort of thing, so the children had a meal.

Barter was a great thing. For instance a dentist friend of ours made a set of teeth for gardening work done for him. It was five years like this. During that time we never purchased clothes in a shop, things were given to us.

About this time Elsie Locke wrote down from Wellington. She was forming women's committees. There was a heightened feeling of militancy and a number of very fine women joined the committees and we held meetings and discussed this and that, things with a politics flavour of course. And we held demonstrations. If anything came up that threatened the little bit we had, we'd hold a demonstration. I remember on one occasion we walked to the Council Chambers behind a red flag which we'd made ourselves, and we draped it over the mayor's chair before the mayor came in. We had to remove it when he came.

The women's committees were all organised for a peaceable reason, to make the women more conscious of what was going on and why, and we did a certain amount of political study at these meetings and we discussed how it was affecting individuals—each woman would give a talk on how she was making out and that sort of thing so we sort of knew where each one stood, and how it was affecting the women. Some women of course—under the influence of their husbands—were a bit disinclined to come in on anything that was a little bit political, but we had a fair number. Then we organised a dance . . . I think it was one shilling to get in . . . and the women's committees baked the supper and we all went up and ran this dance—we had to pay for the band of course and the rent of the hall which was very cheap in those days—and there we sold literature and gave talks and somewhere about 1932-33 a conference was organised in Wellington and this was a mighty effort. The Wellington women held raffles and that sort of thing and they raised enough money to hire a house and a woman to cook meals for us and two delegates came from each centre, or one from some centres, and we all met there and had lectures morning and afternoon. How on earth it was done I don't know, but it was a wonderful effort. But although women were having such a bad time during the Depression, they were still very loath to be implicated in any political action. So these committees were to strengthen them, and give them a bit of knowledge. We had a nucleus of women who were active.

Women had to keep their families on 29/6, the set relief wage then; there was three weeks of that and then one stand-down week. For women with children—I had children myself—there was no hope of buying clothes. The footwear was mostly canvas shoes which were very cheap, half a crown or so. For the small children, the depot sometimes gave out shoes, but there was one case that I knew of in a depot I attended where the husband took the shoes and sold them for drink. I can remember we all at St Peter's Depot in Ferry Road used to get away from the heater in the winter time and let these kids with no shoes sit around with their mother. They had no shoes. They had blue feet. And they'd come there without breakfast—they came to get Weetbix and that sort of thing as a hurry-up breakfast. I can remember one cold morning, I had socks over my hands—bikes of course were the means of transport—and I'd biked up to the Depot and I had these socks on my hands and one of these little children—she had one in her arms and two clinging to her skirts—fell over in the mud. I remember wiping the child's face with my sock. Poor little kiddies.

I also remember coming home from the Depot and being given beetroot. Evidently someone didn't like the beetroot and they'd thrown them in a drain and another woman and I went down to the drain and picked them up. We just couldn't afford to pass anything by. I used to have thoughts of stealing. I remember seeing a bread cart outside a shop and just wondering if I could just walk past and steal a loaf of bread. Before I'd had my children I'd studied a bit about vitamins and diet and that sort of thing and I wished I hadn't. It was a question of eating what you could get. You got various things, sometimes a bag of flour, always white bread, and rice—sometimes a pound of rice would be given to us, so you had to eat these things you see. We were very seldom given meat. They did give some frozen flaps, but they were really unpalatable. One man said his dog wouldn't eat them. When they were thawed out they had a very fusty smell—it was very inferior food. But I can remember mincing it up all the same and eating them. Milk, we kept going on milk. But of course all of the 29/6 had to go on food, I mean there was nothing else possible. Boot repairs were done cheaply at the Depot and later on, 1934 I should say, they were getting suits of clothes for about two pounds.

We used to think that we could get through all right, if we didn't have another child. Well, we did have another child and it was then that the effect of the Depression became apparent. People unknown to us came with baby clothes—I think that child had more baby clothes than any of the others—and on the job the husbands pooled together and one man's wife who was having a child, she'd tell her husband she didn't have much so and so and did I have much so and so, so we exchanged. Then I went into Essex Home . . . I think I paid 10/- or something. I only paid 10/- to have that baby. The matron came round and said did we have anything to give her, and we just hadn't anything to give her. But in there I met a woman who was having her fifth girl, while I was having my fifth boy. I gave her what girl's clothes I had in my collection and I remember her husband biking down to our place after I came out of the home, with a cabbage. This sort of thing you see happened a lot; the feeling was there, the mutual aid

National delegates of the women's committee of the Unemployed Workers' Movement meet in Wellington 1932, their gathering paid for from the proceeds of raffles and dances. Photo Connie Beardsley.

sort of feeling had grown. Whatever we had it was useful to someone else.

If it had gone on much longer I think that we would have become more militant. As it was, this feeling of mutual aid was there. It was not there in the beginning, in the beginning people were out for what they could get for themselves and they'd push in at the Depot to get in first in case something extra was going and that sort of thing. Later it was quite different . . . people had real feeling for one another.

Mostly the aid depots were organised by churches, the sort of humanitarian ministries which have a depot and things were given to them, things were brought in by people. Of course, anyone who had a job at four pounds a week during the Depression was well off, really well off, because prices were low. The vicar of St Peter's organised this depot that was in my area. You were asked to go to the depots in your district of course. There was a tendency for people to go round all the depots and try and skim the cream. That was in the first when everyone was out for what they could get, but that was stopped, more or less. I suppose some people still did it but where possible you were asked where you lived. And that was about all. You just went in with your bag and they gave you what was going.

My husband had to go into hospital for a goitre operation and of course that meant that I was right down on the Benevolent Committee. The Depot did what they could but of course it wasn't enough. I had no income to pay. In those days you went to the Hospital Board—hundreds of people went to the hospital—we went at 8am in the morning and I was one of the fortunate ones of course, being "B". I was called fairly early and I used to get away by about dinner time. But you milled around—you know that courtyard in the hospital where the ambulances used to turn in—you milled around in there and then finally your name was called and you went in before the Board and they asked you all sorts of searching questions about whether you belonged to any Friendly Society or Benefit to give you relief, and if they found you didn't, they were usually not bad. They gave me 12/6d worth of groceries and it was quite good to me really, the Benevolent Committee. And then they built underneath the boiler house or something in the hospital. There was a passage along there and you went along to a hall, and this was the Benevolent Committee.

A Mrs Green came down to inspect our house of course to see that we were not hiding anything from them. We had a piano which we hung on to, but she didn't say anything about that. She saw the place as it was. Actually our house was sub-standard, it had been a bach and we'd gone into it with the idea of perhaps altering it one day or building another place. But of course things got worse and worse so that she only took one look at the place and she could see that ours was a case of necessity. So I was on that for about a month. They also gave me a week after my husband came out of hospital and he went back to work, but really that was quite a good period for us. There were hundreds of people going to this Benevolent Committee as well as their Depot—people who had no income.

I did buy a stretcher bed off Calder McKay's on time payment and a man used to come and collect the money and it was very difficult, we just hadn't enough, and he brought the manager along and they were going to take the bed and I defied him. I said the bed was to sleep on and I defy you to touch it. So it was left. We managed to pay it off, but I suppose you couldn't blame the firm—they had to make their way too.

I can remember a woman whose son was going to the Depot and she must have known it. She chucked off one day and said to me "Look at them with their sugarbags, fancy going asking for bread." She had no realisation.

The people on four pounds a week were in clover, they really were the aristocracy of the working class. But their attitude in the main was stand-offish. Of course here and there it was good, there were people who realised and helped other people, but in the main people didn't like the unemployed. It took a long time for people to realise that all sorts of people were unemployed.

Few clothes were bought, hand-me-downs from friends, and friends indeed. I remember I had a friend who was in a job and her husband was in a job and she handed me all her last year's clothes so that I always had something to wear. It didn't always suit me but it was something to wear and that was all you could hope for in those days. And for the children, when grey trousers came into vogue, people used to hand me these grey trousers; suits would be out but for small children you could cut up the legs and so I clothed all the children with grey trousers. And that's how we got along.

Our children were fortunate, I think they had a better time. They were lucky that we lived in this place then, where it was sandhills and lupins and they were able to make their own fun. The environment lent itself to large scale paper chases, huts and a miniature golf course the children made. They made their own amusements. They couldn't go out at all, you couldn't afford to take children on trams you see without any money so there were a number of children there and I formed a Pickwick Club and they did lots of reading in their Pickwick

A different sort of queue. Sir Arthur Newsholme and representatives from mothercraft clinics around Wellington gather at Sir Truby King's house 1933. Not everyone had to clothe themselves through the good offices of the relief depot. Photo Alexander Turnbull Library.

Club and I encouraged them to write little essays, do drawings, make up poetry, and that sort of thing. We finally held a concert, in our sitting room, where there was a window box and we had a graveyard scene from "The Bluebird". Some adults came to this and gave us some money and we took all the Pickwick Club to the gardens on the proceeds of this. Just these small things.

Where there were unemployed children going to a district, where there were a number of employed people, there'd be a difference in clothing, but in our district it was mostly working people and a lot of unemployed so that there wasn't much difference made at school and it developed in the children a sort of do-it-yourself thing. I can remember somebody gave my boy a model aeroplane and he couldn't get enough money for a tube of secatine and out of a boot box he made a sort of little peep-show and I didn't know this but he went round the neighbours they told me afterwards singing . . . he couldn't sing at all, but he sang, pretending to be a gypsy and he had this little peep-show you looked in. And the other children gave him a penny and when he got enough for his tube of secatine he was finished—he'd got what he wanted. That sort of thing was rife among children, they made their own pleasures. They didn't feel the Depression as much—the adults felt it more.

The Depression was also very bad for teenagers, they were among the people hardest hit by all this. There were no jobs for them and they walked round doing nothing as there was nothing for them to do. And it was hard for their folks to keep them. At the age when they should have been into a job of some description and having the discipline of working—they had nothing. I used to worry that the Depression would go on so long that my children would come to this age but luckily it lifted soon enough for them to find employment when they reached that age.

We did send one boy to secondary school during the Depression, he went to Tech. I remember we had a number of coats, but the suit trousers had worn out. A number of coats were given us and somebody had given me a paper pattern and out of the back of the coat where the seam came down I cut this tailor's pattern and put a completely new seat in the pants, and there was the coat to go with it. He went to school in that suit. Books were on loan from the Tech, pupils biked toTech, of course it was hardly any extra cost at that time. Footwear was the trouble. One time I'd said to our three at school, if I'm not home when you come home to lunch, don't go back to school, and they didn't because we had no bread. You see there was no credit, you couldn't get things on credit, so you just had to go without. I sometimes had to go to the Central Depot; they didn't welcome me, they said you go to St Peter's, it's your depot on Thursday, and this was about the Monday I think, and I said I know but I haven't any food. They said there's been an increase, your husband's now getting two pounds a week. So they did give me half a loaf of bread and half a pound of butter and something else, I just forget, and I remember biking up my path and the children said hooray, hooray for a meal. And we had this bread and butter and they went back to school quite happy.

I can remember the parson of St Peter's asking me while my husband was in hospital, did I have plenty of furniture, did I have enough beds, because all sorts of things were given to them by people who were employed. Although many employed people didn't approve of the unemployed, they did give to the depots. So I assured him I was all right for furniture. On the way back from the Depot, I always had to take one boy on the back of the bike as well as the load of Depot stuff on the front. It wasn't too far, but there was usually a head wind coming back and it was quite a hardship. I remember some men working on the road as I was biking along against this east wind and one of them said to me, "You'll kill yourself Missus," and that's how I felt too.

Charity Breaks Down

There's the one about the fellow who went up to the Hospital Board to get his handout and they gave him an old flap of mutton and the fellow behind the counter says to him "Well, that'll keep the wolf from the door."

"Keep the wolf from the door!" the chap answered. "We dragged him in months ago and ate him."

There was a story going the rounds at the time in Lower Hutt. I suppose it was true because it was widely reported in the papers—although that's no guarantee come to think of it—about a fellow who had tuberculosis. He couldn't get work, he was too sick, but he had a wife and kids and he couldn't see them starve, so he went and stole something or other, something quite trivial, I can't remember what. He got caught and the Magistrate sentenced him to three months. So he was locked up, but that didn't help much because his family was still starving. His wife was a very proud woman. She wouldn't ask for charity, and she sold every stick of furniture they had to feed those kids. By the time the neighbours found out about it they had nothing, absolutely nothing. They were just sitting in an empty house eating out of a communal pot with their fingers. I think that brought it home to a lot of people who, up till then, thought that if you were unemployed or had nothing or were living in poverty then you had only yourself to blame. The community reaction was profound shock. The Mayor and the Council got busy after that and set up relief depots but it took something like that to get them cracking. A lot of people just closed their minds to what was going on around them until it was forced on their attention—and even then some of them just looked the other way or pretended nothing was happening.

Those were very hard times in our house. My mother put up with a lot of hard times . . . We went to the Council Chambers and we stood outside from half-past seven in the morning till half-past two in the afternoon. We were granted 2/6d worth of food. We got a loaf of bread, half a pound of tea, half a pound of butter and there was something else—I forget what

Photo Alexander Turnbull Library.

it was—and because I was young and the man behind the counter a little bit of a flirt, he gave me a tin of treacle. That was supposed to be a treat, and I always remember going home with this large tin of treacle.

At the time, when they said half a crown I said "Is that all?" And one great big pot-bellied policeman said "Some people are never satisfied." I turned round and I was just going to say something to him and my mother grabbed me, she thought I was going to say something you know . . . I was just going to say to him, "You, you great big pot-bellied thing, you most probably wouldn't know what it was to go without a feed." But anyway, my mother grabbed me and saved the situation.

And another time when we were waiting outside the Council Chambers, she slipped past the police and got up to the door of the Council Chambers and opened the door and spoke in front of all the Council and she was arrested and she had to attend Court. She said to the Magistrate about young girls with babies going without food and she said they didn't know how they managed. And he said "Yes, but you don't class yourself as a young girl do you?"

"No," she said, and took off her shoe, and there was a hole in the bottom and she put her finger through the hole and said "If I have a man to care for me, and I have to wear shoes like this, how do young girls get on that have nobody to care for them?"

She was a battler, but how she managed. I'll never know how she managed.

I remember taking a suitcase and going to the Hospital Board to get rations of bread, sugar and tea and meat and things like that, you know. I don't know if we got any help with the rent or not, I can't remember.

These depots did have a setup in at the shops and things where you went with a card. There was one in particular, an upstairs place. They'd planted a chap at the head and we went up there and we had to show him the card, stamped and verified and questioned, and you might get a handout, half a bag of coal—you had to put up the other half of the money to get a full bag—but you could go there and get the half and if you could get it on the handlebars of your bike, OK. There was a lot of skullduggery went on in these places. We even had a so-called doctor. I believe he had been a doctor but was struck off the roll. He used to get women coming in with complaints, and there was all sorts of things went on there. You know how gullible the worker can be. But I'd been up there and I was talking about Harry McDonald who was at the Lewis Pass—he was pretty well up in the Communist Party then—and he led a deputation to that place and they complained about the skullduggery that was going on. Now it so happened that somebody burned the place down . . . as a matter of fact it's well known it was the jokers at work in there, they burnt the place because they were scared of getting found out.

I can remember the time when my mother went there for meat, there was even horse manure on some of it. They used to throw it on the floor! They had paper down—but me mother kicked up bobsydie about that place. She reckons it was contaminated and there was some sort of germs on it and she reckoned it was horse manure. Anyhow, there were all these sort of things going on there.

I was married with one kiddie when the Depression was on although I wasn't on relief straight away. I kept my job for a while but eventually I was out of work and I used to go down to the relief depot in Christchurch where Hancock's brewery used to be. It's where the buses park now, but in those days it was a relief depot. I used to get twenty-eight bob a week and fifteen bob of that went in rent so I only had thirteen bob to buy everything else. It didn't go far, even in those days, so I used to have to go and get a grocery order and that to make ends meet. I remember one time I went

ueing for relief 1933. Photo Alexander Turnbull Library.

down and they gave me a handful of rice and a little parcel of meat. I took it home and my wife unwrapped it and she almost had a fit. Even the bloody dog would've turned its nose up at it. It was high—rotten.

That was the sort of thing that happened, but if you knew someone it was a different story. I remember before I was out of work, I was getting about five quid a week which wasn't a bad wage in those days but even so things were getting a bit tough, that was in 1930 or '31 I think. So I said to the landlady of the house I was living in at the time: "How about me renting out half the house?" and she said, "I don't care, go for your life." So I took in this bloke who was actually on relief. He always paid his rent on the dot so I didn't have any complaint, but I was in his kitchen one day and I saw into his cupboard and it was absolutely packed with food. All sorts of tinned stuff, and sugar and stuff. I was very surprised but I didn't say anything. It was none of my business. But here was a bloke who was on relief and he had stuff in that cupboard that I couldn't afford and I was in work. But I found out later that he had a friend in the relief depot and there was quite a racket going. All the good stuff was going out the back door to friends of the blokes in charge, and the people like me who were going in the front door were getting the rubbish. All through the Depression that bloke lived like Riley, on charity. He always had good meat. It was a good time if you knew somebody.

The Wellington relief depot used to be in Buckle Street and they used to have clerks behind grilles, but the grilles only went up so high, about six feet, and after that they were wire netting up to the ceiling, about ten feet. They had to do that. People would wait for hours at a time in the queue and then get to the grille and be told by some snotty little clerk that they couldn't have relief. The people used to get pretty wild and they'd grab whatever was handy and let fly. Too many clerks were getting damaged—that's why they put up the wire netting.

Well, as a single man you might know a girl who worked in a restaurant, in a hotel, and friends who could give you a few bob now and then, something like that, ask you to their places. It was more or less a regular thing you'd get invited to somebody's place on a Saturday or a Sunday or both days and so on and so forth. Well, these people were exceptionally kind to all of us, they'd go out of their way to help you.

The organisation that I remember most vividly is Buckle Street, right under the carillon on the corner of Taranaki Street and Buckle Street. It's now a military establishment. We used to line up in the yard there and go through and get detailed on to sustenance or whatever it might be, or relief work . . . checked for anything that you might have in the way of money, how you were living, signing this, that and the other form. There was almost a batallion of check-out boys to see that you weren't getting away with more than you were entitled to, that you *were* really on the poverty line. The hostilities that developed between these people—some of whom weren't bad, and those who were unemployed were something to make you weep at times to see the opposition. A man would get mad behind a counter, he couldn't get the answers to the questions and he had to get the answers to the questions and the poor devil on the other side who was to give the answers was scared that not only would he put himself out of a chance of getting a little bit better out of life, but he might do harm to somebody else and so on and so forth . . . and they used to have police handy in behind the screens sometimes to come out and scare people, ask them a few questions, take them down to the station and so forth.

You might be asked what you spent money on the previous week. They might have found out you'd been down to the Smith Family and you'd got a pair of boots for nothing. The Smith Family ran a show in the Town Hall. The relief people would check up on everything. You couldn't have a radio; if you could afford a radio you didn't get relief. Of course you couldn't have a telephone, anything like that was just barred and so in those days the popular thing was the crystal set, people had their own crystal set.

The Depression hit some sorts of people harder than others. Those on the lower incomes, who were originally on lower incomes and consequently who were paying rent, paying furniture off, and so on, were getting evicted from their homes. The result was the Unemployed Workers' Movement set up throughout the country and in most places anti-eviction committees. Groups were put in houses to protect the people from entry by bailiffs, seizing furniture and so on.

On the relief jobs themselves you found all categories of people. Surprising the people . . . medical students who couldn't make the grade, lawyers, accountants and so on. I worked with a couple up Northland way in Wellington, Wilton block, a famous unemployed stronghold. Quite a militant team of workers up there actually. We were battering down the sides of hills for new roads; the Wilton Road was originated during the unemployed days . . . wheeling and pushing barrows and pushing stuff over the side . . . excavating under City Council administration and City Council foremen and so on. Very few of them liked the job because they knew they were there to carry out a job with exploited labour.

I remember one chap who used to come to work in a reasonably decent suit and the crowd used to poke fun at him. And I used to feel very sorry for him because he was a man who'd had a pretty decent sort of life and had come down in the world and he'd fallen a bit further than a helluva lot of us had fallen, that was just the point, and I used to try and make that point to the chaps. And it took on with quite a lot of them and it got a lot easier for him in the finish. But the last I heard of him he'd committed suicide, he just couldn't take it. Of course it's understandable when a man has been in a good position and comes a thud like that.

I remember once I was collecting some meat and potatoes from the mayor's relief depot in St Andrew Street, Dunedin, standing there with my sugar-bag along with a queue of unemployed. In front of me was an elderly woman dressed in a long black coat, land shoes, no stockings and with two of the most prominent wisdom teeth I've ever seen. The mayoress, a stately person, was handling the meat issue. She handed this woman a forequarter of mutton. The woman looked at her meat and said loudly to the mayoress: "Hasn't any of these shops got any arses?" Meaning, of course, hindquarters. The mayoress turned red and the crowd laughed.

There was no jolly work, couldn't get a job anywhere. Then we went down to apply at the Labour Department for a job and they wanted to send me away up King Country. I said "Oh yeah, you do?" and they said "Yes."

"That'll be the day," I said.

"You come back this afternoon and we'll give you your rail ticket and you can go up there for a job."

I went back in the afternoon and I told them they could keep the flippin' ticket. I said I wouldn't go. The joker said "Oh well, you'll get no work." I said "Would you go up there and leave your wife and kiddies at home? You send the single blokes up, I'm not gonna go. You can do what you damn well like." So anyway they ummed and aahed there for a while and they told me to come back in a couple of days' time. I went back and they gave me a job—I think it was that particular time we had to go away out to Seatoun way, and I got two and a half days a week. I was on the side of the roads cleaning out the water tables.

When I got down there I met a fella called Wally Locke, he was the foreman on the job, and he reckoned the jokers carted more dirt out on their boots than they did with their shovels, so he reckoned he was going to have the jokers throw their shovels down and go in the drain and out the drain, in the drain and out the drain, and everytime they came out the drain they had to scrape their boots off. He reckoned that way they'd carry more dirt out on their boots than with their shovels. That was funny that was.

For that I got twenty-six shillings a week. It wasn't enough to live on because we had rates to pay and all the different things. I used to get a day now and again on the Council to pay off my rates and a day now and again if we wanted a pair of blankets or a pair of boots. One day I wanted a pair of boots and I went down to the Relief Depot to get these boots and they gave me a ticket to go and put in a day's work and I told them I wouldn't. They said well, you'll get no boots. I said "I bet I do." So I went straight across the road to the mayor, and I asked him if it was a fair go. I said I had to go and put in a day's work and you know jolly well I'm in the band and we hold concerts to get money for the Relief Depot, and now they want me to go and work for them. He said "You go back and tell them straight that they've got to give you the boots without a day's work. In fact I'll ring them up." So he rang them up and told them he was sending me back and they were to give me these boots without working for them.

I got a lot of jobs by myself too. I went haymaking one time and I had a job for the Automobile Association. There was two or three of us, we used to look after cars for the night on the streets. We had tickets with numbers on and we'd tear them out of the book and write the number of the car on and in the butt of the book and we'd look after the car, and when they came out from the pictures and that they'd give us the ticket back and often they'd chuck up 6d or a shilling or whatever they thought it was worth to look after their car. One night I spent the whole night from 7 o'clock till 11 o'clock on one car. He came in about 7 o'clock and I thought oh well, I'll get more, and I never had any more come in and when he came along to collect the car he said "Thanks very much." I said "Hey mate, you ever read those tickets?" He said "No." I said "You read it, and it says there that the patrolman wasn't paid by the AA, we just relied on what the owners of the car would give us." So he dived his hand into his pocket and gave me sixpence. And I stood from 7 o'clock till 11 o'clock at night for that.

I was on looking after the cars one night and a chap came along and he wanted to know if I knew where one of me other cobbers was, fellow called Dixon. I said he wasn't there and what did he want him for. He said "I wanted him to go haymaking tomorrow." I said "Well, what about giving me the job?" He said "Yeah, okay. I'll pick you up in the morning here at the Post Office, but you'll have to bring your own eats because there's no house out there anywhere and you'll have to take your own drinks." I said that was all right. I knew he was desperate for a fellow so I said "What are you payin' an hour?" He said "1/6d." I said "That's no good to me. The job I was on today they paid 2/6d an hour, supplied all the tucker you could eat and all the drinks you could drink." So he said he'd give me 2/6d an hour but told me not to say a word to any of the other fellows about it. I said "Okay."

So when we got out to the job at Linton, the first thing he said to me was "Can you handle horses?" I said "Yes." "Well," he said, "You get the horses in and use the sweep to sweep all the hay up the hill and they'll stack it." So he told another chap to go and catch the horses and this fellow said to me "What's he paying you?" and I told him. He said "Right." I said "Now don't you say a word that I've told you." He said "No, but I'll have a talk to the other fellows and we'll get the same too." So at the end of the day when the job was finished they hit him up for the half-a-crown an hour and of course he went a bit crook then, but he had to pay it.

Then he came in one night looking for this joker Dixon again, and he wanted a tree cut down at one of his houses. He had three or four houses he was rentin' and this tree was hanging right over all the footpath. So anyhow I met him after tea one night at the Post Office, and he took me down to the house and showed me the tree and he said "I'll go in and ask the people where they want the stuff put, and we'll see if we can put the tools in their shed." So as soon as he got out of the car and went in through the gate, I had a look and he had a saw and slasher and axe in the car so I grabbed the saw and up over the fence and up the tree and when he came out I had it all cut down. He'd told me it'd take me a day's work to cut it down and he said he'd give me 14/- for the day's work. When he came out he said "You didn't take long." I said "No, course I didn't." So when we got back up to the Post Office he offered me 1/6 for my work and I wouldn't take it. "Not in my life," I said, "you told me you'd give me 14/- for cuttin' down the tree—you said it'd take me all day. It don't matter how long it took, you still give me the 14/-." So he coughed that up in the finish for that too.

And then another time I had another job too shifting some bricks for an old Brethren chap. When I finished he offered me 5/- for shifting those bricks, and I wouldn't take it. He said "Why? I can get any amount of unemployed chaps to do it for that." I said "Yes and you're just the kind of miserable old cuss that would too. So I don't want that. If you don't give me 14/- for the job all those bricks will go back and then you'll have the job of shiftin' them again." So anyhow he paid up his fourteen bob too.

After bailing up Gordon Coates the Christchurch relief workers forced him to agree that something had to be done. That something turned out to be the distribution of the surplus money accumulated by the Municipal Electricity Department, after its conversion into groceries. The unemployed, distinguishable by their cheap Japanese sandshoes, queue for their meagre dole. Photo Frank Renwick.

Backblock camps for the outcast, the superfluous,
reading back-date magazines, rolling cheap cigarettes,
not mated;
witnesses to the constriction of life essential
to the maintenance of the rate of profit
as distinct from the gross increment of wealth.
"Dominion"
A.R.D. Fairburn

I'd worked as a very junior clerk in a plumber's office and as the Depression developed slightly, things got tight there and I was put off. Then I spent quite a lot of time looking around Christchurch trying to get another job comparable to what I'd been doing, but they were few and far between. So finally, being unable to be kept by my parents, I applied for a job on relief. Being single I was forced to take a job out of town which made it impossible to look for a normal job. The first job I went out to was on a farm property right up in Ashburton Gorge. It was draining swampy paddocks and we had to dig huge trenches and then go into adjoining paddocks and get stones, boulders as heavy as we could handle, toss them onto drays, cart them back and we built these stone drains round these paddocks. It was the middle of winter, and I must say that I wasn't very hard in those days. We used to get 25 degrees of frost of a morning. We were quartered in the shearers' quarters which we didn't think very much of but I realised later that they were a palace compared with some of the places I was in. This went on for about six weeks until finally, in trying to lift some heavy boulders, I strained my back very badly and was put into bed for a few days and I was unable to continue the job and had to return to Christchurch. I forget whether I was still given relief while I had a bad back or not, it's too long ago to remember now.

There was an office set up in Christchurch where you had to queue up and give all your particulars and they took the facts and they offered you . . . well, not too many jobs, but for a single man there was only the one option. They called it I think the 9A Scheme and it was working on farms helping farmers out. Up to a point it was all right but the farmers generally treated us like animals and in a lot of places we were quartered like animals. I can remember one place in particular on Banks Peninsula with a converted cow byre and it was just full of fleas and most uncomfortable to live in, and the food was atrocious. The place was crawling with maggots.

Another job was when we went fern cutting on Banks Peninsula, then road building on Banks Peninsula—that was quite a tough job actually. There were no such things as kanga hammers or pneumatic drills, it was purely a matter of sledge hammers and rock chisels of some sort and then blasting what we couldn't hack out. Then finally (this was of course over a period of two or three years) I went to Eyrewell State Plantation to plant trees. Back-breaking job it was too. There I got appendicitis, went back into Christchurch into hospital and after I recovered from that I went up to build the Summit Road along the top of the Port Hills. All these were relief jobs of course. Then I went cutting timber and helping to stack timber at the Burwood Plantation. Finally I got a job in the Botanical Gardens raking up leaves and keeping the gardens tidy.

All this was very degrading and very heartbreaking because one couldn't get a job. I was going with a girl who is now my wife—we were going together for eight years and would have loved to get married, but it was just impossible while this Depression was going, and we just had to put up with it. The people we

to Alexander Turnbull Library.

to Alexander Turnbull Library.

worked for, they varied quite a lot. Some of the farmers were quite all right. A lot of them were so badly off themselves that they weren't in a very much better position than what we were. We struck cases like that. There were other cases where farmers obviously had plenty of money—they were just using us for cheap labour and we rather resented that but there was very little we could do about it.

There were so many of the public affected by the Depression that those who were affected were sympathetic. Those who were not affected rather looked down upon us as no-hopers, that sort of thing. They didn't take into account that with single men especially you were sent to work in the country, in fact you had little option. While you were fit anyway you were sent to work in the country and there was no chance of looking for a job or finding a job in town while you were in the country, so it just became a vicious circle.

Married men applied to the various depots for food. They invariably seemed to have a sugarbag to put it in and they used to queue up at the hospital and the Salvation Army for example, and other relief depots and be given half a pound of sugar and a few mutton chops and a little bit of this and a little bit of that. It was just pure charity and very degrading, but what else could one do . . .

A brother-in-law of mine was very well up in the working class movement and he went up to Lewis Pass and he organised everything along with a Glasgow chap named Smith. They even had their own newspaper after the style of the Russians. You wouldn't believe it but they had a committee for food, a committee for everything, there was no work done because they were going to try and stick to the 1928 Public Works Act. Of course nobody turned to, and the foreman couldn't handle it so the head of the Public Works, he was sent for and he had to hire a cockie's dray to get across the river. And he got there and he came in and had a look and he sat down on a table and he could see this newspaper. Oh Jesus. But my brother-in-law, Harry McDonald, he up and said "Excuse me, the men object to you sitting on the dining table." And the Public Works man jumped up, "You won't have it much longer!" and off he goes. The men organised themselves. They held the whole camp up and refused to work. And they walked into Christchurch, all of them from Lewis Pass. You know, they couldn't hold it themselves, it was shut down. That camp was never opened until the landslide of the Labour government in '35. Then that camp was opened at sixteen shillings a day at that time. But they never opened that camp again—they couldn't, the chaps all marched in. They refused to work in what they called slave camps.

When I first went to Hamner Springs, they had a big marquee and it was winter time, snow and everything, and we actually dined with hats on. There were kerosene lamps hanging up just above the tables. After about a week or two you can imagine it was a quagmire. They got carpenters out and built an outside framework over the marquee and put shingle down. You know the army dixie?—we had one filled with hot water. We were issued with army plates, pannikin and so on, and you could have as many blankets as you liked, black army blankets. We all had just the one plate, and as you got meat and potatoes and things, then you had to go and wash the plate for your pudding. You can imagine that. There were 80 men in that camp and you can imagine what that dixie was like—just scum. We were under canvas, 28 degrees of frost and we were in tents.

The work was cutting out trees. The trees were planted by prison labour prior to the 1914-1918 war, that was a good while before, and their technique at that

ef work camp at Glen Wye, Canterbury August 1932. Forty-seven men made their home here while they constructed the Lewis road to the West Coast. Photo NZ Free Lance

Aka Aka," reported the Auckland Weekly News, "the men bathe in the drains and wash in a horse trough." Nothing so vulgar in evidence when this official party visited a relief workers' camp at Akatarawa. Photo Alexander Turnbull Library.

time was four feet apart so the trees of course take up. We came along and cut every other one out more or less, not if it was a particularly good one. We were in gangs. There were returned soldiers from the 1914-1918 war employed there as gangers, just one or two, and we were spread right through the block. And there was a chap watching for anybody lagging behind. And if chaps were good, we had to get on to them to slow up. There was a chap there, he was from Birmingham, and he was particularly good—we even blunted his axe—but he still bruised his way through, he couldn't take it easy, he was rugged. He used to bath in the snow, rub himself down.

Some chaps who couldn't keep up, they were sacked. At Hamner Springs all we got per calendar month was our keep and three pounds.

Then I worked up in the Port Hills. That was another kettle of fish. Two days a week, if you had one child you got half a day, so you worked two and a half days; you worked two days one week and three the next. And we used to have to go up there and there was a Scotsman chap and he was a staff-hand with the Public Works and had a whistle. We used to have to walk from St Martins right to the summit. In the winter time it wasn't particularly easy and we had a few arguments with him. We had to walk way up to the top and then if the conditions were so terrible that you couldn't work, he'd blow his whistle and we'd go back. But this time we stayed in our tents and he said "Everybody all bale out." It was snowing. Well, there was a chap, a schoolteacher out of work, he was a kind of spokesman for us and I remember we walked up and we got to the top, and this schoolteacher put it to the chap in charge from Public Works. We went to this fellow, Hunter was his name, always wore a cloth cap. "The men here think we shouldn't have walked up, that you should dismiss right now." And Hunter said "I'll decide who goes, I'm the one in charge" and he turned his back on us. There had been plenty of snow falling and it was snowing again and one chap threw a snowball, got him right on the back of the head—a beauty, knocked his hat off.

The chap said "It'll do you good, the walk." I said "You're in an entirely different category. You're a man on a salary or a weekly wage" (they were paid monthly in the Public Works then). I said "You've got coal and heat at home, and food—some of these chaps are going home soaking wet, they've got nothing to dry themselves." He didn't even think of that but it made no difference, he had his instructions.

We were not long married when the first dingy grey huts for single men arrived. This was the depth of the Depression: 1934. Conditions for many people were desperately hard. In all towns and in many country centres food and clothing were being distributed to the destitute. It was the year of the sugarbag. Every week you'd see the father of a needy family trudging to the centre with his empty sugarbag for his handout. Such a handout would be anything anyone could spare for destitute families. We all sent in any clothing we no longer wanted: anything we could spare—say, a bag of potatoes, a few vegetables. But seldom, if ever, any money.

And near us the camp for unemployed men continued to grow. By the end of the week fifty of the dingy huts stood on either side of our house, alongside the main road. Conditions were grim. Organisation was poor. The huts arrived; the men arrived—the toilets did not. It was more than a week before they arrived and were put up. Can you imagine it?

Each man did his own cooking on a small stove in his hut. He collected his firewood from the plantation, or from anywhere it could be found. He had to carry water for cooking and washing from the creek. The men got five shillings oto Auckland Public Library.

ad construction by unemployed during the Depression. 1930's Akatarawa. Photo Alexander Turnbull Library.

a day, that's all, and the work they did was cutting off corners and improving the roads. It was pick, shovel and wheelbarrow work except for one contractor who had a team of draught horses and tip drays. He was a nice old man. He liked horses, he did *not* like men.

Politics were in the very air in those days. The old contractor was a Tory—the men were Socialists. He was able to make a point about human nature, however. After the first few months a system of contracting by small gangs replaced the wages system for some of the men. I well remember the old man's glee when he told us that for all their Socialist ideas they kicked out anyone who couldn't pull his weight in the gang—and this was quite true.

The old contractor loved his horses, he understood them and treated them well, and I'm sure he got the best out of them. They grazed on our land, for a small amount per week, and were worked and spelled periodically. He kept a neat little booklet and had his own idea of the past tense of "arrive". It would read: "Grazing for March. Bonnie, Prince, Nell, Darkie, Sall—March 18th. Sall went off and Punch *arrove*. Grazing for April. Bonnie, Prince, Nell, Darkie Punch—April 15th. Darkie went off and Nance *arrove*." And so on.

Later, another contractor turned up with a Model T Ford truck, antiquated even then. I can still hear the old affair rattling past with its half-yard or so of gravel—shovelled by hand and off-loaded with a hand-operated hoist. Some weekends as many men as possible would pile aboard the old vehicle and go to Dunedin for a brief reunion with their wives. That old truck was the only transport for the whole camp.

A rule insisted that no wives or families were to be in camp, but one little man evaded the rule. He apparently left everything to fate, and arrived at the nearest railway station with his family and all their wordly belongings—which weren't many, believe me.

By pure chance, my husband was at the station when the train came puffing in. Everything—including three young children—was piled into the car. They were not allowed PWD huts (that's Public Works Department huts); they weren't allowed to camp on the public roadways, so the stranded family asked permission to camp on our land. How could we refuse? So tents were pitched and a fireplace made, and that was "home" for the family for an entire year.

I can't think how that woman managed the cooking and washing for three children—but manage she did, and the children were always clean and neat. When she wasn't gathering wood or carrying water, she was sewing or knitting. When my own baby was born six months later, she brought in a pair of blue booties she'd knitted for me. Within a week of arrival, she'd dug a strip of land and planted lettuce and cress seed. Later she added a short row of sweet peas and some marigolds. The sweet peas were not a success, because one of the horses developed a liking for them, but the marigolds flourished. That summer they made a bright orange patch beside the little tent .

Those children of thirty years ago: where are they today, I wonder? Do they remember, and perhaps tell their own children stories of the time they lived in a tent for a whole year?

One of the most tragic aspects of the Depression was the number of skilled men who were destitute, really destitute. When we were building our house on do-it-yourself lines, on two different occasions carpenters walked in off the road to ask for a job. We couldn't afford to employ anyone. One of them, however, seeing how my husband was using his saw, showed him the right way—long easy strokes instead of short fussy ones. He has never forgotten.

One man at the camp was a cabinet-maker—a good one, but not good at shovelling clay. He had a wife and young family in Dunedin and, perhaps more than most, he was sorry for himself. At weekends he made a few extra shillings doing carpentry jobs around the district. Also, in his spare time, he made some really beautiful ornaments: portable lamp-stands, trays, little wooden calendars—you know, the kind of thing that you alter every day . . . but no one bothers! One small table of his I remember particularly—it was not more than a foot square, all made by hand—carved legs and so on—and really beautifully polished.

One evening he asked us into his hut to see them and I remember feeling rather uncomfortable, wondering if he would perhaps expect us to buy something. But we had no money for that.

Those Depression years were, I think, especially hard for young people, ready to leave school but with no jobs to go to. At least two of the men had sons with them, young lads of fifteen or sixteen, living in the huts and working with picks and wheelbarrows. Another man was an Italian, inevitably called "Mussolini" by everyone. The main occupation at weekends was gathering wood, but this man would go long distances and I can almost see him yet—a big strong man—trudging up the road past our house on a winter's evening carrying a great branch of a tree across his broad shoulders.

A very necessary man in a camp of this sort was the blacksmith. He was kept busy dressing and sharpening those picks, and I'm sure by the end of the year he was an A-grade wheelbarrow mechanic. When the old forge, though still in quite good order, was written off by the Public Works Department, my husband bought it for fifteen shillings and it is still in use on the farm today.

The job of improving the road called for clearing away several pine trees at one of the corners: Two of the men, really skilled bushmen, felled them with axes only. Perhaps the Public Works Department didn't have a saw, or maybe the men just preferred it that way, I don't know, but they made a quick efficient job of it. The old knotted wood was of very little use, it was quite unsuitable for burning in the little stoves, but there were thousands of cones. All the men arrived with bags and buckets to collect them, so there would be warm huts for at least a few nights that winter.

A collection was taken up by the men to buy a wireless, and finally a second-hand set was bought for five pounds. Like the truck, even for 1935, it was a strange vintage model. It was set up in one of the huts, but before long it went wrong, and my husband was asked if he could fix it. Luckily it was only a loose valve and he was able to do so: my husband won quite a reputation. The radio very soon went wrong again, however. This time it was much more serious and we took it to Oamaru for expert attention. My husband's reputation diminished.

Today, when I look out my window, I can see very little of the old camp site because the trees have grown tall, hiding my view. But thirty years ago I could see it all. I saw it on grey days, with the rain pelting down on the little grey huts—a desolate scene indeed. But on an early spring morning with the sun rising red behind them and every little chimney puffing smoke up into the still air—it was almost picturesque; on the surface, anyhow.

1935 drew to an unlamented close. It was election year, and the night of the election we had some of the men in to hear the results on the radio. As the Labour victories piled up into a landslide it became a night of triumph and hope for them, beginning with the good news announced by Bob Semple (that unconventional and irrepressible politician), that they were going to get a Christmas bonus.

There was a popular song about then with a gay, lilting tune called *Happy Days Are Here Again*. For these men, and for others like them, it was about time.

I was at high school in Wellington and the school used to back up onto the town belt up on Mount Victoria, and the teacher used to take us on what he called "nature rambles". I think he was just bored and wanted to get out of the classroom. There were a lot of unemployed men up on Mount Victoria doing useful things like making scenic walks through the trees and other important capital works. And this old swine of a teacher used to make a special point of pointing out to us men leaning on shovels whenever he saw one. "This," he would say, almost trembling with rage, "is how the taxpayer's money is being wasted on layabouts who won't help themselves." I noticed he never said it in the hearing of anyone who had a shovel or some other blunt instrument handy.

From *First Day on the Dole* by Jim Forsyth

A keen biting wind whistled through the gorge as the truck rattled and bumped its way along the rough road. Frost sparkled with a brittle brightness from the cliffs on both sides, but to the twelve men huddled in the truck the beauty of the gorge at dawn held no appeal. Jammed closely together, muffled to the ears, cold, miserable, speechless except for an occasional curse when the truck hit a pothole and the resulting bump jarred the spine spitefully, we sat, eyes half-closed, looking at nothing. The sideboards of the truck just reached high enough to give to our backs the minimum of support with the maximum of discomfort. Beneath our crossed legs lay a bunch of slashers which kept up a monotonous metallic clatter as we jolted along. We'd left town at 6.30am, and had been travelling for an hour.

This was my first day on the dole.

The truck slowed down, stopped with a suddenness that jarred us to the teeth, and the engine spluttered and died. No one moved. Like good soldiers we awaited orders. The door of the cab opened and one of the largest lumps of humanity contained inside one skin I have ever seen, erupted on to the roadway.

Our foreman.

I hadn't seen him when we boarded the truck in town; he'd given his orders from within the cab, and it was not yet daylight. I disliked his voice, it was too offensively hearty and senselessly profane, the voice of a bully. Now I saw him for the first time in the cold light of dawn, and came to the conclusion that his appearance matched his voice. He was tall, and broad-shouldered, pauncy but powerful, his face puffy with a network of thin blue lines criss-crossing his red cheeks, and eyes like slits.

He stood in the middle of the road and roared one word: "Out!"

Painfully we rose and dropped from the truck in turn. Standing on the ground, we tried to restore circulation by stamping around and flapping our arms. I looked down at the river running through the gorge and the gorse-covered flat between, and I heard the man next to me say: "God!" The foreman turned to him: "It's no use asking Him to help, He doesn't work here." Then he guffawed loudly, looking around as if seeking applause. My toes itched.

Still stiff and sore from our jolting journey, we slid and tumbled down the steep bank to the flat, where we followed the big man as he threaded his way between the gorse bushes till we reached a small clearing. In the centre of the clearing lay the cold remains of yesterday's fire. There we stood while the foreman presented each of us with a slasher and punctuated the presentation with crude, supposedly humorous remarks.

"Don't lean too hard on that one, it's liable to break," he said to one man. To another: "Don't work too hard or your missus will be disappointed tonight." Each remark was followed by his horrible guffaw.

On receiving my slasher I took off my coat and moved towards the nearest clump of gorse. I was cold and intended to get the circulation moving in my miserable body. I started to chop at the gorse. That is when I struck trouble. There was a bellow from behind and I turned to see the foreman striding towards me.

Wondering what I had done to enrage him, I said: "Why, what's the matter?"

He stopped and turning to the others grouped around the dead fire, he said with mock amazement: "Did you hear that?" 'What's the matter?' he says."

Photo Rotorua Museum.

I looked at the group—they were grinning, a somewhat sickly grin, I thought. It was evident that they had seen this happen before.

He turned to me: "You start when I say so, not before. Get that into your thick skull my lad." My circulation started to move with a vengeance. Before I could reply he said in a much calmer tone: "This job's got to last a long time yet. Can you play five hundred?"

The irrelevance of the question had me bewildered. I shook my head, confessed I could not play five hundred and awaited the result. It came with a sneer: "And you don't play poker I'll bet. You Scotch are too bloody mean." He laughed loudly and the laugh was echoed by three of the men.

I looked coldly at the men then with an effort to keep calm I said: "*Scots* is the word, and I'm not mean enough to take my pay for nothing."

He looked at me for a moment, his mind seeming to search for my meaning, but it evidently eluded him. "All right," he said. "If you're so bally keen to work, cut enough gorse to start a fire and keep it going." In company with the others I did as he said, then started to work slowly away from the fire. The foreman and the three who had laughed settled down to their game of cards around the fire.

We gradually worked far enough to be out of earshot of the four card players seated round the fire, and I noticed my companions looking at me from time to time. Eventually one of them, a thin white-faced lad, looked in the direction of the card players, then turning to me said: "I say, Scotty, you want to be careful what you say to Big Bill."

The others stopped and looked at me.

"Why?" I asked.

"He's liable to report you, and you can be suspended for a week, or maybe two."

That hadn't occurred to me: and the thought turned me a little cold. I had a wife and four children, and even the small sum of 32/6 a week helped a little. However I had started, and had to keep up a bold front. So I forced a smile and said: "Look, laddie, I've worked beside men who'd have suspended Big Bill from one hand, tied him in a knot and thrown him away." I was thinking of my old pals in the Wairarapa and the Rimutakas: Jim Murphy and his mates. "In any case if he reports me I shall report him. He's not paid for playing five hundred, and if you people have any guts you'll back me up. Then things might be a bit happier around here."

One of the others spoke: "He's got a lot of friends back in town."

As coolly as I could, I replied: "So have I," and carried on slashing gorse.

That of course was very far from the truth, and I was a complete stranger and knew no one in town. Much later, when it didn't matter any more, I learned that everything I said had been repeated to Big Bill. My bluff may have worked because I heard no more about it.

As I worked that day, I studied my companions. Most of them had been on the dole for over a year, and the effects were plain to see. There was a visible hopelessness in their words and actions, their thoughts stretched no further than the day when they'd receive their scanty reward for grubbing gorse. Instead of looking forward, they looked back in retrospect to the good jobs they'd once had and the money they'd once spent. Their faces in repose were creased with anxiety, and they seemed to be fighting a mental battle, trying to hold on to something which was slipping away. I came to share that anxiety, but strange to say I never gave up hope or faith in New Zealand. Rightly or wrongly, I pinned my faith on my knowledge of those cool, practical fighting Diggers I had seen in the Sinai and in France, and I thought: "They'll find a way out of this mess somehow."

Later, much later, they did. But in the meantime: I was on the dole . . .

One bloke who I had no recollection of, but he told me he had worked on the face of the Ngaio Gorge at one stage—I was working with years later on the waterfront. He came out of school, onto the labour market and couldn't get a job; there were simply no jobs. His recollections of the slump were principally of what a wonderful time it was, because he was free of the burden of not having to work. He said that even when you were desperately poor and hungry there was a sense of festivity. He pressed this fact on me greatly, that you didn't really need to care about work every morning and when you were put on relief this was a very bad thing, because you did have to turn up somewhere. But he found that there were ways around this too.

He described in great detail how for the enormous amount of men working on the excavation at that field at the top of Mount Victoria, there was only one boss. There was a little shed, where the tools were kept, and trucks would arrive with the surplus tools from some other job at a later stage in the morning. The thing to do was to get on the tail-end of the queue for the first lot of tools as the picks, shovels and wheelbarrows were handed out first and then they got down to smaller and smaller tools, there were spades of varying depths and sizes and finally at the tail-end of the queue you'd get a tiny fork or trowel. If you got one of these you couldn't do much excavation with that and you had a light day. All the blokes who knew did *get onto the tail-end of the queue. There were so many blokes working, no matter what tool you had to work with, it was a comparatively simple matter to get somewhere out of the vision of the pannikan boss, and perch yourself amongst the pine trees. The pine trees had been planted around about in the 1920s, they were very low and you had to stoop down to get among them and if the boss wasn't up your end then you'd go down to Evans Bay and spend the day swimming, and get back again by five o'clock in time to clock in and return your tools again. He used to describe this in terms of high hilarity and had absolutely no qualms of conscience about it. He didn't feel he'd been chiselling, after all, he said, he hadn't asked to be born into this crazy society, where there were not enough satisfactory jobs for everybody.*

He did mention one day when he did do a day's work on the end of a trowel. He was given a particular part of a clay face to dig and he said it was a tremendous satisfaction to him to see a piece of this clay face being dug away—slowly, slowly, but eventually getting there. Even though he could only take little spoonfuls of dirt away from it, he did actually achieve something. He was always agitating to have that playground used publically. It was still part of the school ground and he was very sure this was only used by the privileged. He had this feeling that Wellington College was a privileged school and work that was done at public expense should be public ground. But the interesting thing to me was the actual work experience, no matter how frustrating, still actually meant something to him.

He used to approach obvious members of the gentility who were working with him on relief. He used to feel desperately sorry about these people. He used to talk about how the way he was dressed meant nothing to him, having no job. He never had a decent suit or a best pair of shoes. He told me about the occasion when he bought his first raincoat—somewhere in 1939. He went into a shop and bought an overcoat, because always up until then he used to wear a sugarbag. This is what one used in the Depression. It had a hood, it was most probably the prototype of the parka, you shoved your head into one corner, you left the bottom of one side sewn up and ripped up one side, and this thing hung all over you. Potato sacks were better in some ways, although it depended on the state of the hem or what the sack was made of. A new one was likely to have a better run-off for the rain and when they started making flax ones, maybe a bit of a wool bale, they'd be much better coverage, but sugarbags did.

Old Bill never thought of actually buying an overcoat. Occasionally there were hand-outs of this sort of thing from Depots and soup kitchens and these sorts of clothes were handed out to the poor, but generally it was little kids who went to these places and men rarely frequented them. You saw a lot of people around shabbily dressed—many, many more than you do now. I mean now, one is aware that there is a partly deliberate revolt against the affluence of one generation by the next: young people indicate their contempt for material possessions, and this was the sort of philosophy that would have been understood by people like Bill. He actually enjoyed the fact that he didn't have possessions and he said how hard it was for people bringing up families. He was single and young and really found the whole experience exhilarating. It developed him into a radical of course. He was aware that had he got himself into a job he would never have thought about political questions very much at all. It would've been the least thing in his mind, and he always says that he probably would have gone from one job to another, but ultimately he would have settled down and into a groove, where he had a comparatively good job. He was the sort of person that would have got some sort of low-grade clerical job, but risen comparatively quickly because of his quick grasp of things. As he says, "I would have turned into a two-bob Tory years ago." This never happened to him, he never developed a materialistic attitude at all. He always despised society.

There were a number of people who used to come along in a bowler hat and briefcase and suit and then put on overalls behind the shed somewhere to work, and take off the bowler hat or hang up the suit on a tree or somewhere, where it would be out of the dust. And they would have their lunch in their little briefcase. And they had to take off their overalls and put them back into the briefcase at the end of the day and they'd dust off their trousers and put on their bowler hat and go home, as if they were going to some respectable job, as far as the neighbourhood was concerned, perhaps even as far as their wives and family were concerned. These people really found it degrading to do this kind of work and Bill used to feel desperately sorry of them. He recognised that as far as they were concerned it was a tragedy. He always said that he only hoped that these people let the tragedy scar their souls. He was frightened that they would slip back into some respectable groove and get a job and the whole thing would be forgotten, a buried facet of their life which would never be mentioned. A lot of people are like this about poverty. The respectable middle-class tends to regard poverty as a sin, some sort of punishment for a wicked thing that they had done.

At the time I had a wife and five children between the ages of six and fourteen and my quota of work on relief was three days per week for two weeks and no work for the third week. On the Friday of the stand-down week myself and hundreds of others paraded outside the boardroom of the Canterbury Hospital Board in Christchurch. This was known as the 'sugarbag parade'. The procedure was to put your name on the muster roll and wait your turn to be interviewed by the Benevolent Committee of the Board who granted you rations from the storeroom. My quota of rations for myself and my family of six was thirteen shillings worth of groceries and a voucher worth two shillings and sixpence for meat from the butcher. This was the amount you received to feed your family for a week. The rations weren't a free gift at the time. You were required to work out the value of the rations received for some local body in the area, in my case the Gardens and Domains Board.

My first job on relief was cleaning out the water races in Paparua County. This work was normally performed by the permanent county employees but perhaps with the idea of keeping the rates down they were granted the labour of the unemployed supplied to them by the relief organisations. The intake for the main races was about two miles beyond Halkett which would be about eighteen miles from the county office in Sockburn. I lived at Hornby at the time and what I had to do was to be at the intake at eight in the morning, which meant I had to push my ramshackle bike seventeen miles all the way uphill carrying on the bike a shovel supplied by the county, a pair of gumboots, reaphook, an oilskin coat of my own, lunch, and a bottle of tea. If you ran into a nor'wester it was just too bad. No break for a smoke, no boil the billy, only your cold tea to drink at mid-day. After working at the job for eight hours I biked the seventeen miles home again. Each day the gang cleaned about one mile of race so that meant I had a mile less to travel each day each way. For all this hard travelling and work I received 37/6 for the three days, my quota for the week. On the third week we were back at Hospital for the sugarbag parade. The water race cleaning only lasted a few weeks and then they sent us to build a golf course at Templeton Domain. That was much better, only a three-mile ride on the bike and no boots to carry. The golf course we made on public land is now the Templeton Country Club. A Mr Blair, a professional, laid out the course and then another man and myself went out to get the course ready. The only tools provided were a horse-drawn mower, a huge roller and an old draught horse, although we got a truck later.

They were certainly grim days. Some of the men working on the Waimakariri River Trust Scheme picketed the job for better conditions and were arrested and imprisoned. An old law was dug out of the statute book which very few people had heard of. They were charged with 'besetting'—trying to prevent people from working. The police and magistrates had a lot of power in those days. A working friend of mine who died recently, a very respected man but a bit of a radical, received two years' imprisonment for having in his possession some large photographs of the Dneiper Dam in Russia. In my opinion the African witchdoctors had nothing on the police and magistrates at the time. I remember too that a gang of relief workers were employed similar to a team of horses at harrowing

Relief workers roadmaking at Karori, Wellington, the Karori cemetery in the background. Photo Alexander Turnbull Library.

Photo Frank Renwick.

with tine harrows on land belonging to the aerodrome at Wigram. But for all that when things were hard, I think I'll always remember from that time the way men who were in great hardship always helped one another if they could.

I well remember in Anderson Park there used to be a great gully down one side of the park and the hills on the other side. Well, a good deal of relief work during the Depression was organised under the Number 5 scheme through the local authorities and they had to scratch up jobs. The more people that could be put to work the better. So the fewer tools they had, the better. You might have a job say in Anderson Park where you might have one shovel for three men, or one grubber to two men and these people would scratch around in this clay and load it into a wagon and instead of having a horse to pull it away to the tip into the gully, the men would push it and tip it into the gully because you could use more men in that way. I well remember when they were making playing fields around Wellington in such a manner that they had to prepare the surface for sowing to put grass on it. This meant breaking it up and normally that kind of thing was done with a chain harrow. I remember seeing men harnessed to a chain harrow when normally you had a tractor or some horses to do this work. So here you had a kind of Volga boatmen kind of situation. Well this isn't wrong *in a Volga boatmen situation, it's* wrong *in a New Zealand situation, where this kind of work could well have been done by machines if the economic system could have been handled*

"They shoot horses don't they?" The horses have apparently already been shot. Men on relief work pull a chain harrow at Petone 1932. Photo W.B. Sutch.

properly. But it wasn't. The result was that any job that could be multiplied by not using tools and not using machines was done so. I saw many other humiliating examples.

If you didn't have any debts, in some cases you could survive. Similarly, if you didn't have to pay rent, you could survive. People who had rent owing to them of course were often in a desperate position. Anybody who'd lent on mortgage of course was in a desperate position too. I well remember lawyers and businessmen working on relief work in the same gang as my father. They were all there together and it wasn't a question of inability to work. My father could probably do the work better than some of the businessmen. On the other hand, I've seen businessmen less well shod on the job than my father—who had some heavy boots. I've seen businessmen working in sandshoes, waiting for their turn on the grubber to do their job of work. They had to report at a certain time in the morning and walk off again at another time and they had to be there all the time, allegedly working. I know one disgraceful situation where there used to be a railway development and people were building cuttings and putting fill into the gullies. This was stopped because it was public works, and all public works were stopped. But the men were there and the Works Department was giving them relief work and they had a gang that they were giving a couple of days' work a week to. They had a lot of rubbish, logs and clay and stuff to shift, so they said to the men "Shift this," and it was shifted over to where the engineers indicated. Then the problem was what to do? The engineers looked around for more work and there wasn't any more so they said "Shift it back again." Here you had men shifting this heap of clay and rubbish from one spot to another and back again. You can't conceive of a worse form of degradation. Those men on relief knew very well that if they went on with the railway cutting they could sweat for something that was really achieving something. Then they would be doing something for themselves and the country. But the just useless shifting of clay from one spot to another and back again was a terrible thing.

Then too the unemployment camps, which I inevitably noticed, where young men and married men were put into these camps in tents. They kept these people out of the towns and to some extent of course stopped a good deal of social unrest by getting some of the active people out into these country camps.

Coats Off With Coates Man Who Gets Things Done

I'd no doubt whatever that the thing to do was to employ all the trained teachers, instead of which of course they closed the teachers' colleges and—frankly—we've never recovered until these last few years. Another interesting thing, too, about the use of funds for employment: R.G. Ridley of the Wellington Technical College begged the government not to sack apprentices, begged the government to pay the employers the apprentices' wages and if they didn't have enough work at the shop to send them to school—three weeks in four perhaps they'd be at school, whatever it was, to keep the apprenticeship system going. Ridley said don't allow the apprentices to be fired, subsidise the employers who couldn't afford to pay apprentices and didn't have the work, let them go to school, employ some of the tradesmen who were out of work to teach the apprentices, and build up a body of skilled men for the future. The government wouldn't take any notice of him and that was a major tragedy. The number of apprentices in New Zealand fell to about 2,500. Now that meant that when the second world war came to an end, there were no tradesmen to train the next lot of apprentices and we've not caught up on that either. This country has imported skilled tradesmen since the war. Now we can't get them and we're very short of skilled tradesmen. You can't overcome a backlog like this.

These were tragic errors.

But when Labour came in they found to their surprise several things in the garden which are not so well known as they might be. For instance there was a 44 million pound credit overseas. No one expected this and it was never publicised because it would have been bad political propaganda in Coates' party. To have the money overseas, and not use it here. Second, the Labour government in 1935 found that there were blueprints for state housing, medical health and God alone knows what, done by Coates' backroom boys, you know, W.B. Sutch, Campbell who became Director of Education, Alister McIntosh who became Secretary for External Affairs, Gordon Wilson who became Government Architect, a whole lot of them who had done blueprints for the future. And they were excellent, they really were first-class. And the Labour party found—I think to its surprise—that an enormous number of the kinds of reforms they wanted were already in embryo, they were there. So I think the Labour Party was shocked.

Coates was a far-sighted man. He didn't expect to lose the 1935 election. He sensed in 1934 that the Depression was over. Coates knew it and saw it and expected with the postponement of the election from 1934 to 1935 that the lift would have been enough to get him in. But of course people have longer memories than that.

Coates had great difficulty in getting his party to do anything. I don't think he was a theoretician, but he was a much more humane man than he was given credit for. He was blamed for the Depression, which was nonsense, it was a world thing. No, Coates knew the thing would come through and he stacked up his overseas balances which were essential for the future. He did a good deal of getting stuff ready for the future . . . you know like housing and one thing and another.

Minister of Finance Gordon Coates takes time off from advising the unemployed to eat grass to watch horses run on it. Photo Alexander Turnbull Library.

HAS THE KIWI GONE CLUCKY?

The Unemployed: "Do, please, hu rry up and do something with that enormous egg."

Auckland Weekly News.

But there were also some very bad things he did. For instance he denied children entry to school until the age of six, which was of course entirely in order to cut out a whole class in primary schools and therefore a whole bunch of teachers. Well that was a terrible thing. There were a lot of things like that, all sorts of cuts. The cuts in salary were quite justifiable because there wasn't the money, but cuts in the spending, it seems to be all wrong. What you've got to do in times of Depression is wisely spend, I think, it's gotta be wise. Just as I think in prosperous times you ought to curtail your expenditure and save. I mean Nordmeyer in 1958 saw that clearly enough and of course nobody would take any notice of him and put the Labour Party in the wilderness. But he was right of course. And Coates too, to some extent.

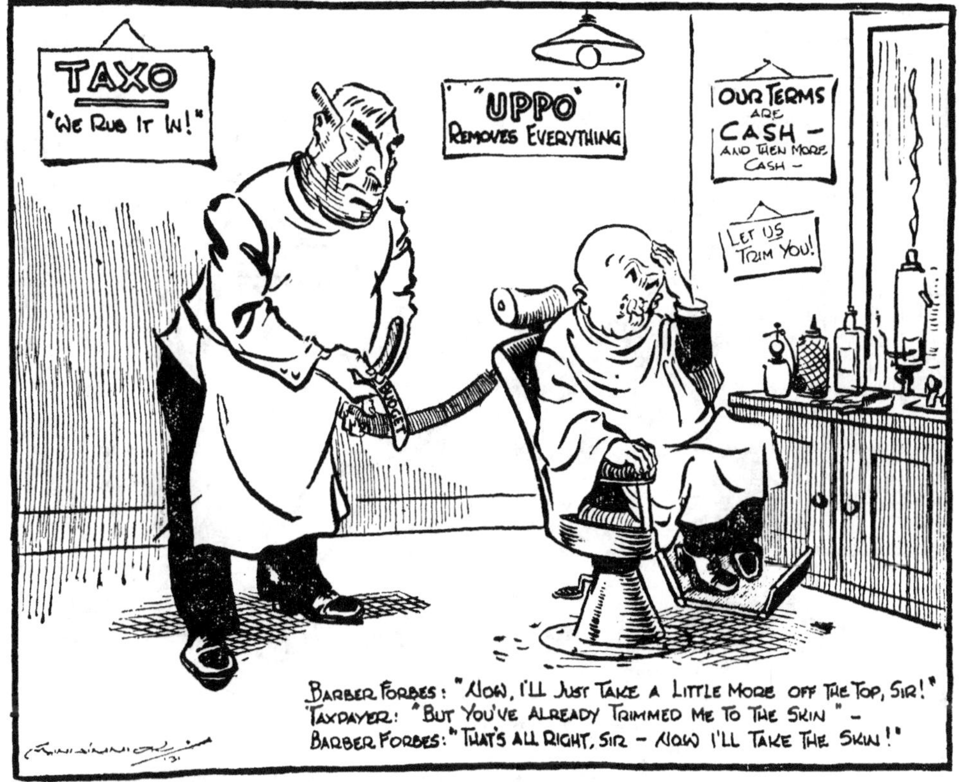

THE SKIN GAME.

Auckland Weekly News.

My mother had taken my sister and I into the city and we had gone to watch a crowd collecting outside the old Grand Hotel in Princes Street. The crowd had collected because they had knowledge that Mr Forbes of the Coates/Forbes coalition government was at that time attending an official dinner. The crowd was angry; many of them were ragged and hungry and obviously there were a great many unemployed amongst the crowd. They demanded that their grievances should be heard and when Mr Forbes appeared on a balcony at the hotel, resplendent in his evening suit, this incensed the crowd—who immediately started to abuse him. Some missiles were thrown and although he tried to speak to the crowd there was no opportunity for him to be able to be heard over the hubbub. He then retreated into the hotel and attempted some minutes later to make a getaway from another entrance. Some of the crowd got wind of this and immediately tried to besiege him in his car. The whole incident had rather nasty overtones, but it gave a very good indication of the mood of the people towards the ruling government of the time, and in particular personified in the appearance of Mr Forbes.

THE PROPOSAL.

Auckland Weekly News

The Coalition (that was the National Party really) didn't know what to do. I don't think they were bad men or anything like that, but they just simply hadn't a clue what to do to handle it. Of course there were relief schemes of various sorts, not very enlightened. The government were not heartless or cruel men; old Forbes for instance I think was a very decent old chap, but I don't think he had a clue. Gordon Coates was rather a fine man and had a lot of feeling for people. But by the end he was was beginning to have some clues, because while he didn't have very many ideas, he had a willingness to listen to ideas. And Gordon Coates was beginning to listen to ideas, to the ideas of people like Bill Sutch. And if Gordon Coates had had a freer hand, he probably—on good advice—would have done many more good things. But of course the Coalition government's idea was that if you had a hard time you just starved it out. There wasn't anything much you could do except starve it out. The Labour Party came in with rather more enlightened ideas, and it meant that they at least had enough enlightenment to get moving, and of course once things were moving then everything started to improve tremendously.

This was not the first Depression we'd had in New Zealand. There'd been several very acute ones, going back all the way. But there wasn't any idea what

1931 the United and Reform parties formed a Coalition government to beat the Depression. Instead the Depression beat them. The alition Cabinet smiles nervously for the camera. Photo Alexander Turnbull Library.

tion results posted on the front of the Evening Post 1931. In the days before election broadcasts or widespread possession of os, citizens gathered here on election nights to watch progress at the polls. Photo Alexander Turnbull Library.

to do about it. Take some of the modern things nowadays, the general control of finance and marketing on a wholesale scale and all that kind of business—that was undreamed of. No one had ever thought of it. There wasn't much that could be done unless of course you did what some of the wild people were suggesting and that was you kind of revolutionised your whole system, something of that sort, which would be looked upon by most people with horror. A Depression was just one of the things that happened, and there wasn't much you could do about it. That was the general idea. Any of the things that could have been done would have been looked upon as a red revolution, shocking.

New Zealanders were very individualistic in those days. Each individual farmer ran his individual farm and he sold his stuff where he could sell it. He had no idea of huge marketing combines whereby all the butter in New Zealand was sold in a lump and so forth with the proceeds shared round. No idea like that. He was an individual. The working-class man was very much the same way. Everybody was an individual and everybody in a sense did his own thing. He had to balance his budget and if he didn't balance his budget it was tragic just as it would be today for me if I didn't balance my budget. There was no idea of a national organisation whereby credit and all sorts of things like that could be manoeuvred and you could keep things moving, even if you were hit hard in some particular fashion. To the politicians of the day, the country was run very much as you would perhaps run an individual business, as you would run your own farm. And of course a great many of them were farmers anyway. Just as you would run your own farm; if you didn't pay your debts of course you were done, you would be off your farm in pretty quick time. So, the same applied to the country and there was no room for manoeuvre. Well, we've learnt a good deal since then.

There was very little in the way of any enlightened action on the part of the government. They were just faced with the appalling fact that they couldn't pay their debts, so "we've just got to starve our way through". And of course any of the schemes that were started by the government were in themselves very small and limited. Although perhaps they should have been able to think in wider terms—as they had in the first world war—they didn't. Of course war was something rather holy—the government couldn't do the same to rehabilitate the country.

People hated Forbes and Coates. I got thrown out of a meeting in the Town Hall for challenging Forbes to come clean about the Ottawa Agreement. The police threw me out, rolling me down the stairs, but no charges were laid against me. I got back the same night and Coates was there, standing at his car, with his hand on top of the car. I can see him to this day, arguing the toss with the unemployed. And he was given as good as he gave. In many ways Coates was an admirable type, he had guts—you disagreed with him, sure, but the point was this that he stuck to his guns. He did finally get in his car and take off. There was some milling round the car, outside the Town Hall on the Cuba Street entrance, but he stood his ground for as long as he could. And he smilingly got into the car and waved to the crowd and they booed him and blurted at him all sorts of things, but he still waved when the car took off. A few missiles were thrown but no harm was done. Coates could live up to that sort of thing.

But Coates had made that famous statement when the unemployed called on him in his room in parliament. He said "You can eat grass." Now I wasn't there, and sometimes a man can make a statement in an absolutely jocular vein and really not mean it, but a hell of a lot was made of that statement.

viceregal visitor, apparently sober that day, chats with returned servicemen 1934. Photo Alexander Turnbull Library.

931 the government, worried by the Depression, called the National Economy Conference with representatives from all political ties. From left: Reform: Hon.W. Stewart, Rt Hon.J. Coates, D. Jones; United: Hon.E.A. Ranson, Rt.Hon.G.W. Forbes, Sir Apirana ta; Independent: A. Wilkinson; Labour: M.J. Savage, H.E. Holland, J. McCombs. Photo Alexander Turnbull Library.

I think it must have been about 1931 when the government closed down the training colleges, people know about that. But most people don't know that they also issued an instruction that where there were married women working as teachers they were to be dismissed. The idea was more jobs for the men. So that cut a lot of family incomes in half because in those days you got a lot of husbands and wives, both teachers. Except there was a proviso: the wife could keep on working if she and her husband went to a dual charge school. I suppose that was cheaper for the Education Department, only one house to provide and all that. The applications must have flooded in. Now here's the interesting thing. A lot of those little country dual charge schools were Maori schools, and quite suddenly the Maori education system, which had had some good teachers of course, but on the whole didn't get the good ones—who naturally wanted to stay in the cities where the prospects were better—well suddenly the Maori schools started getting the cream of the teachers, and they just leapt ahead. A lot of people think that the Labour government stirred up Maori education when it came to power in 1935, and no doubt it did. Money poured in, more equipment and so on. But it had the manpower there, first-class teachers who'd laid the groundwork simply because the government had pushed them out into the backblocks as part of a shortsighted economy measure. It's an ill wind that blows no one good.

Forbes and Coates—I remember them, Forbes in particular, I actually met him. The Duke of Gloucester was out here visiting, just before the war, and he was entertaining him. A couple of thousand of us went to the government buildings and we nailed Forbes up there with the police who were there that night, and Forbes was confronted with our demands for more groceries. Forbes was nailed up there and he couldn't get out of it. And he said "How much would that cost?" Well the chaps said "Well you're the prime minister, you ought to know, have an idea."

"Oh well, we'll have to do something," he said. But we forgot about the lift. It was in the background and the cops thought of it first, opened up the lift and Forbes just went back, into the lift, gone . . . but we each got 7/6 each. And they went to the MED, which had two thousand pounds at that time, surplus, and they cleaned the whole thing out. I can remember everybody bringing a sugarbag—and they just cleaned out that place. We were three or four deep and all we could afford were sandshoes, trousers were about four shillings a pair, and the Japanese sandshoes were a couple of bob.

I met Coates too. There were several delegates from all round, Dunedin, Christchurch—we went up there and he made a very unfortunate—for himself—remark. He said "Well, gentlemen, if you people haven't got a home to go to, I have." Ooh gee whizz! My wife's father was the first one up. He said "We also had homes, until you took them away from us." Coates was there until about ten o'clock at night and they really gave him the works, and he couldn't get away.

People like Forbes and Coates couldn't cope with the Depression. They would be trying to fit in with the orthodox way and they didn't have the brains—or if they did they weren't allowed to use them—to alleviate the whole position. They wouldn't have a show, but you expect leaders to be well-versed in that sort of thing.

The Forbes/Coates government tried everything in their power in the early thirties to do something about the Depression. But they couldn't do much because the associated banks gave them their marching orders. And the government didn't have much imagination so they didn't know what to do with what little power they had. Towards the end they got a bit desperate

JUMPING TO CONCLUSIONS.

Auckland Weekly News

and they started doing funny things. One of the funniest they did was to bring the Governor of one of the Australian states over on a visit, 1934 I think it was, bread and circuses, make people forget their problems a bit. The whole thing turned out to be pretty abortive because this bloke was, well, he used to drink quite a bit more than was good for him. Anyway, part of his tour took him through the North Island by car, and at one small town he was to be given a bit of a welcome. They had a platform all rigged up in the local square or whatever it was, with the mayor, all the local dignitaries and then along the front the school kids. It was also one of the very first live broadcasts done by, I think it was called the New Zealand Broadcasting Company in those days. So anyway the governor's car pulls up and the governor gets out, and decides he's got to go to the lavatory, so away he goes down the road to the municipal gents about fifty yards away. But the mayor was a bit shortsighted and he saw the governor's aide standing by the car twiddling his thumbs and he got it into his head that this was the governor, so away he went down the steps and grabbed the startled aide by the hand and pulled him up on the platform. And listeners at home heard stage whispers: "That's not the governor." Well the mayor wasn't only half blind, he was very short-tempered and he said, quite loudly: "Well, where is the bloody governor?", and a little boy in the front row piped up: "He's in the dunny," and just as he said that, the governor must have flushed the lavatory because there was a sound like Niagara Falls from the municipal lavatory. So that attempt to divert the population from their troubles didn't quite turn out the way it was planned. Didn't do Coates and company any good either. They got turned out the next year and Labour came in.

Don't Just Stand There Do Something

We shall come, the unemployed,
The disinherited of this earth,
We shall come into your temples
And your marble halls of mirth.
We shall come as you have made us,
Ragged, lousy, pale and gaunt,
You, the House of Have, shall listen
Unto us, the House of Want.
We are measuring the weed-chip gangs
That stretch from coast to coast,
We shall come, us, the rightless,
Us, the God forsaken host.
We shall come in all the madness
Born of hunger, pain, and strife,
On our lips the cry for vengeance,
In our souls the lust for life.
We shall swarm as swarmed the locusts
That on Pharoh's kingdom fell,
And sling your politicians
And your damned police to Hell.
by an anonymous worker 1932

In the days of the 1920s and before, unemployment was a characteristic of New Zealand and each trade union tried to look after its own members by giving them some kind of little payment when they were unemployed, keeping a list of them and trying to relate them to any jobs that might be going. If you had a job to offer you could ring up the trade union secretary and say "Who've you got on your books?" This meant that each trade union was adjusted to its own members, and those who became unemployed, well you could try to care for them. But when you had massive unemployment and much of the unemployment was not of men that belonged to a trade union or women that belonged to a trade union, it then became quite outside any method of a trade union movement as a whole, looking after them financially first, and secondly because they weren't members of their particular fraternity. The result was that there was no organisation representing the unemployed as such. Now quite clearly, when you have unemployment, working on a job . . . unemployed men working on a job, even if there are 30 jobs around the town, you've got a dozen men on each job or 20 men on each job or 30 on each job and they talk among themselves; they form a little job team and they may have a job delegate

GENTLEMEN'S
TAILORS

and they decide on their days off. But they'll meet and the job delegate will go from one to the centre and you could have a full meeting of all the unemployed in a particular town which is quite unofficial, no trade union, no rules, but just a discussion about what they should do . . . this was the Unemployed Workers' Movement, beginning on a job basis and meeting from town to town. It gradually became unified with a secretary and president. Their main objectives were to secure better conditions for the unemployed—better tools, better rates of pay, better rations where rations were part of the relief scheme, fewer people sent to the unemployment camps, eliminating the married men, not sending them to unemployment camps—aims that were all related to improving job conditions just like an ordinary trade union. That is, you would not call the movement itself a radical movement. But associated with it was of course the radical political movement which was to some extent on the Labour Party side and to a greater extent on the Communist Party side. You've got to remember that the Communist Party which started activity in this country early in the twenties, was quite a powerful party idealogically, I don't mean in numbers, but there were a lot of people who were very very sympathetic to the Soviet Union and there was a lot of political discussion going on in the country about what was wrong with the capitalist system. So you had the party saying strongly it's imperialism, and they were really trying to say: well we must go further than just ask for better job conditions. They might say it's up to the government to provide full-time jobs all the week at standard rates of pay. They put an element of extra strength into the unemployed workers' movement and indeed they gained a lot of sympathy because, not being based specifically on a trade union but on a political organisation, they could of course associate with the unemployed quite easily rather than the trade unionists (who couldn't even pay the trade union secretary) trying to do much about it. The Communist Party made a fair deal of progress in the thirties and it was acceptable because it was part of the general ferment of discussion. But a bigger party in numbers that existed in the Depression days was the Social Credit movement, particularly the Douglas Social Credit party and they said quite clearly: the show hasn't got enough money to go around, so let's make enough money to go round. And there was this form of preaching, first of all based in the small farming areas, particularly in North Auckland and the Waikato, then the towns. There were in the 1930s much more wide-ranging co-operative discussions on how to cure this thing. So you might have the Unemployed Workers' Movement and the Communist Party and a number of the Social Credit Party and the Land Leaguers all meeting together to discuss how the Depression problems could be cured.

The Unemployed Workers' Movement was part of this general ferment, but in addition to that they would organise processions and on their day off (and there were plenty of them) they might march through the town with banners, very orderly, no need for any police to look after them—they had their own very quiet arrangements. These processions would bring to the attention of the public the thousands of unemployed, their slogans were very reasonable. They might wait up in parliament grounds, they might send a deputation in to see the minister. They might talk on the street corner—talking allegedly from a soapbox—about their grievances, which were very real. So what you had was a constant up-welling from below of the unemployed workers as a movement. Now, I must add this, that occasionally when the politicans came around at election time to discuss with the people what their platform was and the unemployed crowded into the hall, then things became a bit noisy and one or two leading politicians found things a bit threatening for themselves. If you had when you were standing on the platform a hooting, hostile crowd, then you might feel that you'd better get out the back way and this occasionally happened. I don't say there was

Communist labour demonstration in Wellington. While the Minister of Labour was receiving a deputation a section of those accompanying it created a disturbance in the grounds of parliament. The melee took place in the shadow of Seddon's statue.

On the beach for the duration. With a fall of export prices by 40% between 1928 and 1931 there was less call for shipping and many seamen, like this group queueing to enter the Wellington Trades Hall, found themselves out of work. Photo Alexander Turnbull Library.

physical violence, but there was certainly hostility of a great strong nature in the air.

I remember a meeting in Latimer Square. It was a very well organised meeting. The men marched off each relief job and marched up the Square and stood there, they filled Latimer Square, there were thousands. When Alec Glass the spokesman wanted to form a deputation and go round to the Council Chambers some of the hotheads said "No, we'll all go round—all go round or not at all." Well of course there were policemen every two or three yards. I can remember them down Worcester Street right down to the Council Chambers there in Manchester Street, in line—I've never seen so many policemen so thick. And of course this was inviting trouble. I mean there had been riots in Auckland and Wellington but there'd been none in Christchurch. And Alec appealed to them. They pulled these hotheads down off the lorry and they finally had the deputation sent round. That was a successful move there. It showed me that a peaceful demonstration, a firm stand of numbers of people against a certain thing, is much more effective than rioting, than booing, than throwing eggs, anything like that, I deplore that. As a result of that demonstration we didn't have married men's camps. In this case, even the police who were there would have had a hard job to quell us all if they'd got started, but there was no trouble at all.

The police were down on the unemployed, perhaps not so much as they would be now, but they were, they were on the side of the . . . it was their job I suppose you might say. I don't remember a sympathetic policeman—there may have been some, but they were not too bad, I think they turned the other eye you know on occasions. But when it came to a public demonstration they were against the unemployed. I remember a case—it wasn't do to with the police but it just showed the effect this unemployment was having on people. There was a paddock of potatoes around the road from us, a large paddock of potatoes belonging to people owning racehorses and were of course as we thought then fairly well off. And people had been going at night and bandycooting. One night I was walking along with a friend and we met two men with sugarbags balanced on their bikes. The men had sandshoes on which said they were unemployed—you know, it was a sort of uniform. And they suddenly got on their bikes and made off at what speed they could down a side road, and as we came opposite the house of this place, the people had been hiding in the hedge and they called out to run after them. Well of course we hoped that the men got away with their sacks of potatoes. It meant an awful lot to the people who were stealing them and didn't mean very much to the people who were losing them—not too much—a loss in profit. Grown-ups were raiding large orchards. I can remember having apples brought to me and I said "Where'd you get them?" and the chap said "I stole them." And I accepted them, I had no compunction. It just shows how deep the need was for survival.

It was very hard on single men, the Depression. They got very little. If they hadn't a home and were on their own it was very tough. Sort of had a demoralising effect you might say by having to live that way. Property became less sacred, but yet, as I say, there was in Christchurch no rioting, no attacks like that. I don't know where the difference lay. Perhaps in the treatment in Auckland. Christchurch might have had a more sympathetic set of relief depots here.

There was a tremendous radicalism amongst teachers in all directions. There were all sorts of projects, for instance we collected money for Spanish teachers in the Civil War. People sent money in to send help to the Spanish teachers. They thought the anti-Franco attitude important, but not too much so, naturally, because they're a conservative group. There was some

This is through no Replys from the Nat: Ex. of U.W.M. for a few months — Comrade ... Wont to wake up

CANTERBURY UNEMPLOYED WORKERS' ASSOCIATION.

Memorandum to all unemployed; read carefully.

Immediate General Demands agreed to by a Mass Meeting of the Rank and File of above Organisation, and round which the Unemployed of Canterbury are urged to make a militant fight.

IMMEDIATE DEMANDS.

1. Equal Pay for Town and Country Unemployed, Married and Single at not less than 14/6 per day; also Free Transport to and from work.
2. Abolition of all Compulsory Camps for either Married or Single Men.
3. Recogniton of Delegates on All Jobs, and No Victimisation of Same.
4. No Task or Piece Work.
5. Non-payment of Levy by All Unemployed.
6. No Evictions of Relief Workers from their Homes.
7. General All Round Reductions in House Rents.
8. Provision for a Free State Insurance Scheme.
9. Full Sustenance for All Unemployed, when and where no Work is available.
10. Unemployed Women to be included in the provisions of the 1930 Sustenance Act on a basis of Equality with Men; also Adolescents, both Male and Female, between the ages of 16 to 20.
11. Free Medical Attention and Aid for All Unemployed Families; also for Single Unemployed Male and Female.
12. First Aid Outfits on each Job, with a competent First Aid Man in attendance.
13. Free Boots, Free Coal (One Bag Weekly), Clothing, and Blankets for All Unemployed.
14. Full Pay for Time Lost through Wet Weather, and through Sickness.

GENERAL DEMANDS

RESIGNATION OF THE GOVERNMENT
FULL SUSTENANCE EQUAL TO TRADE UNION RATES OF PAY.
RESTORATION OF ALL CUTS IN SALARIES, WAGES and PENSIONS.
WORKERS!!!—Rally round these demands. Organise on the job. Demand your Rights. Show your Solidarity by Standing By Your Comrades.
ALL IN FOR A MASS DEMONSTRATION IN THE NEAR FUTURE.

West, Print, 314 Oxford Terrace.

Chinese thing we collected for too at one time . . . I can't remember what it was now, some minor matter . . . it seems minor now.

There were 1500 to 1800 teachers unemployed. Classes were big, expenditure was low, wages were cut, five-year-olds were kicked out. The total expenditure on education in one year was two and a half million pounds. They're spending more than that between Monday and Friday of every week now. Most people find that hard to believe. The cut then was fantastic. You got nothing. For instance you had to keep a work book but you weren't supplied with one. I think this is a very petty example, but when you're forced to keep a work book and they cut out your half-crown to buy the bloody thing when it's always been given to you, this gets your goat. Chalk was also rationed. You used to draw your chalk each day from a box. There was no money for repairs, no money for building. There were God's amount of kids about, that wasn't the problem. Oh no, the teachers were radicalised because of the conditions. It was really and truly a Leninistic trade union situation. They were radicalised because they were getting such a raw bloody deal. Graduates couldn't get a job, the training colleges were closed, the lecturers were turfed out, there were no new teachers going to be trained, and there were kids coming on. Everything was cut. There weren't as many inspectors, there were as many departmental officers, the education boards were cut, there was no material, in fact the material situation was so bad in Wellington that they wouldn't send it out to the schools and if you had the sense to go along and ask for it and take it away in a bag they'd give you paper or paints and so forth. They really had nothing, it was really grim. The more conservative patriotic ones said "Oh yes, but we must stick by the government." The others said "Boo hoo to that mate." For teachers in New Zealand to take such a stand at that time was not only unprecedented, it was alarming to many people. But the conditions were bad. There was general bad feeling.

It got to such a stage that there were empty rooms and big classes in the rooms that were used in the schools, but outside teachers were picking weeds out of the gardens. I know of two young teachers on unemployment who were keeping the playground in order two half-days a week for their ten bob or whatever it was they got. They were ready and able to work but teachers had their work rationed. They were willing to go back to work and of course that wasn't allowable.

The police during the Depression were very good, very decent. Well they were themselves on the edge of it. They got the cuts, they were hard hit too. I was tagged by the cops all over the country, there must be a file big enough to fit in a wheelbarrow about me, but they were very good, they were very good indeed, and they were very decent.

They handled demonstrations reasonably well, unless they were over-provoked there were very few broken heads. The riot in Auckland was a pretty sad business and it was so unexpected, but I don't think the police were so bad there. The Wellington business was a funny one, that was a peculiar business the Wellington riot. A strange thing, hard to understand what exactly happened. Some ratbag says "Up the street" you see, and they did. They went up and they broke some windows and overturned a car or two and unfortunately one of the cars they overturned and knocked about was Payne's, the Stipendiary Magistrate's own car. He was on the bench next morning. Some of these chaps had bolts with wires through and some of the ratbags threw pepper into policemen's eyes, and they got time, they got a pretty bad time.

But there was considerable fear. Rioting's a very ugly thing. But actually the rioting didn't really get going, which was interesting enough. The police were around about and then for a week there was real hubbub. I thought I'd go down

OFFICIAL NEWS OF STRIKE.

Wellington, 15th July, 1933.

National Strike Definitely ON!

NATIONAL ORGANISERS' REPORTS.

Comrade BELLARBY visited

Masterton.—Promised support under way.

Palmerston North.—Under way with Mass Meeting for support.

Levin.—Full support promised.

Wanganui.—Mass Meeting Tuesday for support.

Comrades CLANCY and KAY visited

Auckland.—OUT. **Hamilton.**—OUT. **Huntly.**—OUT.

Gisborne.—Deciding to-day. **Wairoa.**—Promised support.

Comrade KELLY reports

Napier and Hastings.—Solider than ever.

Hutt.—Mass Meeting on Monday. **Johnsonville.**—Balloting to-night.

Wellington.—Consolidating position daily.

Organisers visiting other North Island Centres.

SOUTH ISLAND.—**Christchurch.**—Standing by for ballot.

West Coast.—Reefton have stated: Ready to down tools, waiting signal District Council.

Dunedin.—Arranging Mass Meeting early in week.

Organisers proceeding South immediately.

Deputation to Minister of Employment this morning, reports:
"Minister shows anxiety and concern over Strike developments."

National Unemployed Workers' Movement.

Whole Organisation behind struggle ! **Organisers in Field !**

The following Resolution was carried unanimously in Hawkes Bay and endorsed fully by Wellington :—

"That this Mass Meeting of Relief Workers of Hawkes Bay, having been on Strike for over a fortnight and recognising that our Delegates have visited the main centres for support in the struggle and that Wellington is definitely **OUT IN SUPPORT** and many other centres preparing to support, we do look upon the statement given to the Press by S. Vella and D. McLoughlin on behalf of their National Union, as misleading and a deliberate attempt to use the biased Press to weaken the Strike. We emphatically condemn their attitude and are of the opinion that they are acting purely as Strike Breakers and against the best interests of the working class."

LATEST NEWS.

Wellington Comrades arrested, rush protests to Minister of Justice.

EMPLOYED WORKERS ASSISTING STRIKE.

Seaman.—Wellington pass Motion at Stop-work Meeting in support of Strike.

Watersiders—Holding Special Meeting on Monday.

Tramwaymen.—Holding Meeting to-morrow.

Napier Watersiders.—Vote £14 Fighting Fund and decide one day Strike in support of Relief Workers' Strike.

Storemen and Packers, Napier.—Vote £10 towards Fighting Fund.

This Fight is YOUR Fight—in to it NOW!

Alexander Turnbull Library.

town and have a look. But they recruited special constables, that was really one of the worst features of it. They recruited special constables and they were of two sorts. Those who went in voluntarily—you'd be surprised at some of the famous radicals for instance who nobody remembers—but I do. Then there were some of the business people, and above all the City Council put the young men on the mat and told them their jobs were on the line and either they recruited as special constabulary or their jobs were gone. Well this was terrible.

The police loathed the special constables and kept them locked up and when there was a real danger of a big riot which built up, you see they had them all locked then in the Grey Street prison, gave them a lecture on what to do and so forth, and never let them out. Police can't stand special constables—they don't trust them you see because policemen know how to behave in a crowd. They know what to do, they're trained, and they can trust each other, they know how to move in formation and how to keep their hands down—you know, put your hand above your head and you're going to have trouble etc. Then when it was all over the special constables paraded up and down the town and of course were called scabs so the whole thing dissolved after a little while. They were issued with batons but they didn't have the special constables anywhere near.

No, it was a very bad show and of course that increased radicalism. I mean if you're working in the City Council as a draughtsman and you're brought in and they say "Simpson have you volunteered for the special constables?" "Oh no." "And why not?" "Well, it's not a thing I feel I ought to do or believe in." "Well we can't see how we can go on employing you in the City Council if you're not prepared to protect its property." So this all radicalised an enormous number of people. All the influences were in the one direction; there were no counter influences, there were no conservative influences.

When the march was decided on people were chosen from all the surrounding relief and railway camps to take part. It took us a couple of days to get to Wairoa, and then we had a truck to get us most of the way to Napier. We didn't walk all the way, only when coming into the major towns. We had meetings at Napier, quite a good turnout, and also Hastings and a few odd places on the way. The local government had spotting planes and police scattered about all over the place trying to find out where the unemployed were, and apparently they missed us for two or three days although we were, in fact, on the road. Just outside of Palmerston North we spent two or three days resting up. At that time the Major Douglas crowd were having a national conference and the unemployed went down there and started asking questions. The social creditors were blinded with science and could hardly answer any. We were very unpopular.

Palmerston North was an interesting occasion. The representatives of the government were there. We had a big meeting outside the Masonic Hotel and they tried to create a riot scene there, with soldiers in the background and machine guns and whatnot. Some of the spectators threw tomatoes and eggs and that, but this was uncalled for by the unemployed because we didn't believe in any unnecessary provocation. The police tried to hustle us about but we formed a very tight formation. We presented our case before the Minister for Unemployment and two of the other ministers there.

We wouldn't let Forbes go until he promised us something. We worked ourselves south. At Levin we stayed in one of the camps, went into Levin and had meetings, also at Otaki we had good meetings and made a pretty quick tour through Lower Hutt, through Haywards, accommodated in tents which the local unemployed had erected for us. The local MP was against us being in the area and took steps to have us removed but on legal procedure he couldn't because we were on private land. We had a few odd meetings.

ing the Farrow marchers. The Gisborne unemployed were probably the best organised in New Zealand. After a successful week demonstrations in Gisborne they prepare to march to Wellington to dramatise their despair. On the way they were met with offers coffee from farmers and the army with machine guns in Palmerston North. Photo Max Riske.

oto Max Riske.

Thousands of Petone and Hutt people gathered around to meet us and hosts of police were around. By the way, as we were coming down we gathered another twenty or thirty recruits and now some more in preparation for Wellington. Abouty forty of us set out and we didn't lose any along the way. We were going peacefully along the waterfronts into Wellington and as we came nearer the police sailed in, tried to divide and break us up into small groups, but we re-assembled again and the Wellington unemployed assembled in mass and held us in tight formation in the centre like a bodyguard, and so we got down to the unemployed rooms in Wellington.

We sent messages to the government, had mass meetings at the Basin Reserve, Fraser and company were there and they tried to bribe us to go back. Jenkins, our leader, was very strong Labour but a fine leader. It required quite a bit of discipline there. With the assistance of the Wellington unemployed and some others we were able to keep the group together, especially the hunger marchers, and eventually we were told that the government had agreed to grant us a free passage back to Gisborne. Indirectly it had quite a big result because the Labour government came in largely through the efforts of the unemployed organisations.

People donated food for us on the way, all types, mostly plain 'tin can' stuff, kerosene tins full of tea and coffee and so on, mostly from ordinary workers who'd come out to the assistance of the unemployed. We carried very limited cooking gear such as billies to cook potatoes. We didn't worry much about butter as long as we had the bread we were quite happy with that. A number of farmers assisted with meat and that was prepared by the local people. Farmers were pretty good. As far as Gisborne was concerned the unemployed organisation had canvassed a very representative portion of the farmers within a fourteen to twenty mile radius. Many agreed within a certain time to donate livestock, cows, sheep and a limited number of pigs. We also organised finance to help run transport and that sort of thing. The farmers were also very helpful en route. They were very hard pushed themselves as well. Some local councils were helpful—Otaki, Levin and one or two others. At Wairoa the local mayor came out and supervised and arranged and chaired the meeting. In a number of places the mayors did chair the meetings open to the public. People were interested because everyone was affected by unemployment.

Gisborne was rather unique among all the unemployed organisations, it was the strongest and best organised there was. Had good leaders, classes, educational, lecturing,committees for various things, concerts, socials, dances; all these other things and the general public and wealthy people used to say: Well we'll go down and see the unemployed and see what we can do. In the canvassing of the business houses there were only about two which didn't donate regularly to help. These two went out of business. People wouldn't buy from them. Farmers also helped, tilled the land and grew crops to be sent to the unemployed. Unemployed went out in trucks to help the farmers do that, and we used plots of land in the town centre for that too. I think we enlisted much more support than we could have in the cities. We showed how the Depression affected their incomes directly and indirectly, and how things going on would only worsen the situation; then they started to think and come to light. In Gisborne the unemployed handled the distribution of relief themselves, and showed you didn't need an army of clerks.

On the march I remember we handed out leaflets and we sent special advisors out from the Gisborne organisation to the various bodies within the camps so they had the advantages of educational materials and so their representatives knew what to do when we got to Wellington. It was grim going for a start but it paid off in the long run. We had a policy on evictions too. We showed owners that it was futile to put people out when there was no one to take over the place, or the next possible tenant would be unemployed too so they wouldn't gain anything; better to have people in there under the jurisdiction of the unemployed

Photo Alexander Turnbull Library.

At the end of their journey—some smiling, some grim—Gisborne hunger marchers in Wellington in 1934 pause for the camera before dispersing to their homes. Photo Alexander Turnbull Library.

organisation so these places would be carefully looked after, and they'd be responsible to the owners of the houses for any damage or repairs, disciplinary action would be taken if necessary against tenants for wilful damage or destruction, although there was surprisingly little.

We didn't have any disciplinary problems on the march. When we approached Wellington there were a few differences, but the majority of us were for going in en bloc and the leadership carried on. The forty of us got on very well. Oh yes, we sang all sorts of songs. At Palmerston North we had our campfires going there. We consistently had lectures and debates, questions among ourselves in the evenings and any problems we had were discussed. A lot of bystanders asked us questions on the way. The farmers often came out to their gates and we'd bring the truck up there. In the settlements a certain number would be told off to break ranks and reply to the questions, and we issued the leaflets already prepared to let them know we weren't out for trouble but just endeavouring to better our conditions. We drew comparisons between the wealth of the country and how we were living, so they could better understand how the wealth could be used, and how the unemployed could be doing something useful, like the use of the Taranaki iron sands.

People must have got onto the telephone or the bush telegraph because they were often waiting for us. A great morale builder, mounting excitement in Wellington. When we got to Lower Hutt there were tens of thousands accumulated, they blocked the streets, and as we came into Wellington they formed a bloc around us too. When the police tried to cut into the march we didn't use our fists or any violence whatsoever, we just let them push us, turned around and regrouped again. We had this planned out in advance. The women were marvellous, they could speak and put their case very well. I think there were four and two or one of them had her husband there too. They were in Gisborne for a week before, selected from the camps for discussions. We kept the numbers to march down to a reasonable size. Originally we were prepared to march all the way from Gisborne to Napier, but one of the truck owners offered a large truck able to carry all of us and our gear, and of course it was crammed. It took the blankets and there were a couple of tents if I remember rightly, a number of us had our sleeping bags and that made it all right when we were stuck out in the open.

A policeman friend of mine told me that after the big riot had been in progress for a while, the military authorities (whose headquarters were located not far from the Town Hall) had been called upon for assistance and that at one stage they had trucks with engines running all ready to go, machine guns mounted, but the drivers refused to move the trucks. I was, and still am for that matter, very sceptical about this story, but my informant (who unfortunately is now dead) insisted that it was true.

There were many sequels of course, including some prosecutions. I think Jim Edwards, president of the Combined Unemployed Groups, was one of those charged. Another one was Mr F.B. Lark, also prominent in the unemployed movement, but he claimed that he was inside the Town Hall when the riot took place and his case was adjourned to a later date. In the meantime a senior Post Office official friend of mine told me that he could vouch for the truth of Mr Lark's claim, although Mr Lark was not known to him except by sight, because he was standing adjacent to him in the Town Hall. Although he ran some risk of incurring Post Office displeasure, he felt that he could not stand by and allow anyone to be wrongly accused (and perhaps convicted) and therefore when the case came up for rehearing, he appeared in Court and voluntarily gave evidence supporting Mr Lark's claim, the charge then being dismissed.

Queen Street on the night of the riots 1932. Photo NZ Herald.

Photo Auckland Public Library.

I was to be the main speaker at the Town Hall in Auckland. Civil servants were to protest against the wage-cutting policies of the Forbes-Coates government. Retrenchment had already ruined thousands, there were fifty thousand unemployed in the land and the numbers were increasing. The civil servants were to march from the foot of Queen Street to the Town Hall. Mrs Lee and myself and the civil service leaders would lead the procession. Never in history was there such a muster of civil servants. The unemployed on starvation rations had gone on strike for a few more crusts. Men hungry, on strike, from homes where wives and families were hungry as well. The lean, unfed, unemployed numbering thousands decided to march behind the civil servants' procession. When they came to Quay Street, lean, desperate, distraught at the plight of their families, they cheered. They had only the will to resist to sustain them. As they cheered, the tragedy of hunger and want in a world of plenty, the human tragedy, was too much for me. I got out of the way as the procession assembled. Each cheer made me cry and sob like a baby. These were the men who had made the world 'fit for heroes to live in'.

I came back and we started the march up Queen Street to be the Town Hall which would hold 3,000, none of us thinking to ask what would happen when the seventeen or eighteen thousand marchers found the Town Hall full and the doors closed. There was an electrical desperation in the air. Too rapidly people had been forced down from accustomed standards, to hunger. I was told that the procession stretched from the Town Hall to Custom Street. Someone among the unemployed threw iron at a window, and yet none realised the explosive content of the thousands.

The Town Hall was filled by civil servants. The secretary of their organisation was called to talk and then it was my turn. Unknown to us, thousands were piling up at the door. Since the hall was full they couldn't get inside. Some tried. They would have battered down the door. Jim Edwards mounted a soapbox to talk. Hunger had made all these men reckless, they had nothing to lose. Someone attempted to force the door. The police resisted. Edwards challenged. The batons were drawn. Violence erupted. We didn't know this in the hall, but as the hungry men rushed across to arm themselves with pickets pulled from the fence of Scrim's mission, the pressure round the door eased, the concentration was on the conflict of police versus the unemployed, and the police had little stomach for the task, for not a family but had some of its members on the hunger line. The Town Hall door swung open and a group invaded our meeting. "There's blood in the street," someone cried. "The police are using batons."

Our meeting became fantastic. A group of women, hysterical—who wasn't at that moment?—came to the platform, opened the piano, and started to sing The Red Flag.

"The meeting is over," I bawled from the platform. "I'll go out and try to calm the crowd."

I took a chair off the stage to use as a soapbox. I've often wondered what happened to that chair. The fire brigade had been brought down to Grey Street, and I had gone out the Grey Street door. The unemployed were pelting them with stones. The fire brigade had no intention of hosing down the unemployed. "We won't use the hoses," they called out.

Mrs Lee and myself decided to go down Queen Street. The mob were on the way down. Some policemen had their helmets under their arms; they didn't want to appear to be against the hungry. I talked to one or two. Down Queen Street we moved. The unemployed were breaking windows and helping themselves. And funny things were happening as well in that tragic moment. One man who intended to loot nothing sat in a jeweller's window, winding up all the clocks.

aging a dress rehearsal for a night of rioting the Auckland unemployed demonstrate outside the Town Hall April 1932, protesting ainst a cut in the niggardly unemployment relief rates. Photo NZ Herald.

One unemployed man found a proprietor removing goods from his window and accused him of not playing the game. Evidently he thought that a riot wasn't complete unless there was looting.

Queen Street was looted from end to end. Law and order were down and out. Men were being marshalled from the navy to patrol the streets. The looters, being ordinary decent citizens moved to desperation by distress, exploded in violence and then just as suddenly disappeared, not anxious to be seen in the street of anarchy, although they would gather in Karangahape Road for a repeat the next night. Mrs Lee and myself made our own way home wondering what solution would be used to against the hungry. Out of the riot would come the slave camps so that the hungry would not revolt against property. If citizens had not been democratically minded they would have had the government out that week.

The circumstances leading up to it are pretty well known—there's been sufficient written for everybody to know that the unemployed tried to get to a mass meeting in the Auckland Town Hall and unfortunately they tried to close the doors when that was full, which wasn't explained to them. The poor police had the job of doing it. The crowd tried to crash the doors and an ugly situation developed. Most of the accounts I've read have been pretty colourful about this—about a rampaging mob charging down Queen Street out of control. Well, they were out of control to a degree, but from my point of view it is rather interesting. Myself and my brother-in-law at that time, for a hobby we sort of messed round the amateur theatrical business and this particular night I was actually in His Majesty's Arcade, and he was either in the box or in the audience somewhere, and earlier, about seven o'clock, we'd seen the unemployed organisation walking up Queen Street and shortly after the performance started—about five past eight—somebody rang the box office and said pull the steel doors across, that there was a mob coming down Queen Street. So we did this and I was looking out there and the next thing I know I hear some breaking glass.

I walked down to the footpath on His Majesty's Arcade and here were two or three chaps belting in the windows of a tobacconist which was on the corner and helping themselves to cigarettes. So, you know, I sort of looked at them and they looked at me . . . they didn't take any notice, they were bashing in and I couldn't stop them so I went back and got my brother-in-law and said you know we'd better go and stand over by the shop, which we did. Well, I never saw any violence, any personal violence, right through that night. They were protesting—they were breaking windows, sure, and they were pretty uptight—but, when we were standing by our windows, two or three blokes came along and broke the windows of the shoe shop next door—well once again we didn't stop them, they took no notice of us, probably they weren't interested in our goods, but I still never felt in any danger, physical danger, right through that whole night.

By the time the thing was finished there was plate glass spread right out to the middle of Queen Street where the tramlines were. But it's the silly little things that stick in your mind—like a taxi charging down the hill (I can't remember the name of the street) and turning left into Queen Street and getting four flat tires within ten feet. And looking down Queen Street from where we were in the doorway of our shop, seeing one of those wire wastepaper baskets arcing over the head of the crowd to the big plate glass window over the island of one of the big stores. The sound of breaking glass is rather cataclysmic you know, it's a horrifying sound. But we walked around and we had one or two friends come and stop. They were looking at it too; I don't think anybody felt in any physical danger except one poor policeman who walked up Queen Street on the opposite side to where our shop was and they lined the tramway safety zone as it was then, and just hooted him all the way up, but nobody offered to molest him. They screamed at him, they yelled at him, they called him everything, but nobody offered to go near him and considering some of the things that have happened since then during protests, you know I've often wondered what happened because they protested, they damaged shops, I know they did, they made a hell of a mess of them and of course the looters came along afterwards, you know the sneak thieves that always come along. I can still remember one woman across the road—there was a frock shop across the road from us, small, fairly exclusive, only about three models of which one model was a two-piece costume. Somebody had belted a hole in the centre of the window, a big circular one, and this woman came along, grabbed the two-piece costume, I could see it quite plainly, and walked away. Five minutes later she walked back, threw one half of the costume back and put the other up her whatsisname. Now I don't know whether she'd tried it on and decided to keep the skirt or the top of it, and what's more I wasn't going to be bothered asking her. But this was the silly sort of thing that was going on all over the place.

They definitely had no one to stop them in Queen Street. They could have ravaged the whole thing, they could have set a torch to the whole thing, but nothing like that occurred at all. They broke windows, there was a certain amount of pinching going on, a lot of yelling and all this sort of business, but it was not terrifying in the sense of being physically threatened, and I stood there from eight o'clock I suppose till two o'clock in the morning.

I *remember the night of the riot, my wife and I were going to go to the Town Hall—there were two well-known Australian piano duettists—the admission was very low and we were both very very fond of classical music and we had decided to go to this concert. As we approached the front doors of the Town Hall, we saw the head of this procession marching up Queen Street. We could hear this man on the apex of the Town Hall exhorting the crowd, and we saw the head of the procession approach the front doors of the Town Hall and we hung back. We don't know what happened or what was said, but we saw the police draw their batons and start to lash out in every direction and the crowd scattered and we ran up Airdale Street, which is opposite the Town Hall. As we ran up Airdale Street we could hear the crowd tearing the picket fences to pieces and we could hear the stones and the roar of the crowd. So we decided that it was unhealthy to go to this concert in the Town Hall. We didn't go, we went up Airdale Street, across Wakefield Street and down Wellesley Street to the Civic Theatre and we went to the pictures. During the pictures that night we heard people come in and call out. We could tell there was something doing outside becuase during the pictures there were interruptions and after they were over we had to walk down Queen Street to the bus terminal to catch a bus to go home, and we could see the glass and the wreckage on the footpaths.*

A particular constable whose name I won't mention, whom we knew, he came up to me and he showed me a knuckleduster and he said "We were ready for the bastards." This was possibly an isolated case because I don't think that all the police were violent but they were probably provoked and maybe in fear of their own lives and they had to take action to defend themselves. But we do know that this particular constable showed us a brass knuckleduster.

My brother who had a shop opposite the Town Hall and whose window was broken during the riot, he was standing outside the shop talking to one of his assistants and they were talking to a man they knew who was quite inoffensive and a mounted constable came up and whanged this fellow on the head with a baton and this fellow was arrested and subsequently got six months because the magistrates were jailing almost everybody if there was the slightest suspicion that they were in any way involved in the riot. I'm not prepared to say what the rights and wrongs of it are; whether the marchers started the riot, or whether the police did—I'm just recounting the events as I saw them and what I heard. But this was a very sad page in Auckland's history, and it's something I suppose that those older people who saw it will never forget. The next morning when I went to open my little garage, I found a special constable's baton under the door. Some special constables apparently had been sworn in the night before and for some reason or another one of them had shoved that baton in under the door and it was quite two foot long, made of Australian hard-wood, and believe me, it was a dreadful weapon.

I remember talking one day to an old man who was at the time the Regimental Sergeant Major in charge of a group of troops. The incident of course involved the riots in Queen Street and his duties were to act more in the sense of aiding the police in the exercise of their duties. But he and the troops that were involved had discussed the whole matter before they were actually called in to perform these duties and they decided that they would intervene as little as possible. In fact he took it upon himself to instruct his troops that if there should be any violence they were not to intervene and keep as far as possible out of the action that followed, particularly any action that was taken by the police. They considered that as serving members of the armed forces, their duties didn't lie in civilian control.

My mother was a cleaner at the Civic Theatre and could get free tickets about once a month and my father had gone to the pictures—I don't know whether he had anything to do with the riots in the daytime—but anyway he took time off to go to the pictures and at half-time he came out for a smoke. At this stage a number of rioters were beginning their rampage down from the southern end of Queen Street up by the Town Hall and were coming down past the side of the Civic Theatre, breaking windows on both sides of the street as they came. On the side of the Civic Theatre was a sweet stall where there's a firm now that sells girlie books and the proprietor of the sweet stall, more for his own protection than from worrying about the massive glass doors of the theatre, got out several tins of Minties and other kinds of lollies and running out in front of the advancing horde threw handfuls saying "We're with you boys! We're with you boys!" Picking up the bonbons and gratefully eating them, the strikers swept past his shop, passed the big glass doors of the theatre and got stuck into the shop—I think it was Milne & Choyce's or John Courts then, it isn't now—that was just immediately opposite the Civic Theatre.

And that was how Horatio saved the day for the Civic Theatre's massive glass doors.

The Depression for me, as one from a good-middle-class bourgeois, bastard family, was when our family felt—as they say—the pinch. In other words, my family had to take in a little. It was *not* Starvation Gully as a kid of 17, which I learned later that it was, to my horror. At that time people just couldn't actually afford to go to the pie cart. This had never occured to me.

There occurred, when I was young, a dreadful strike in Christchurch. The Working Classes—damn it!—became discontented with their lot. They went on strike! And I, as a 17-year-old student, went and joined the voluntary police or whatever, and they issued me with a tin hat (god bless me, of which I got heartily sick when I was really grown up), and an armlet and a cudgel, and I was put to

After the 1932 riots special police guard what remains of the stock of a tobacconist in Queen Street, Auckland. Photo NZ Herald.

Shop fronts in Queen Street were boarded up the day after the riots in 1932. If the billboard is to be believed sensations at the races were more newsworthy than rioting relief workers. Photo C.G. Scrimgeour.

work because the desperate villains were rising against the established order which it was my duty as a bourgeois, middle-class, bloody ignorant little fool, to defend.

And so, with my tin hat, my armlet and my baton, I went out to defend what they called—and always have you know—Law and Order. That's what the Establishment have always said. It was winter, and it wasn't too warm at all—it was bloody cold. I defended the Sumner Causeway because all these militant workers, the first thing they were going to do was blow up the Sumner Causeway. Ooh, that's the target for tonight! But the sausages we cooked ourselves at three in the morning, they were jolly good, and not a sign of a militant worker.

Then the next piece of defending law and order I think I had to do was when I used to ride up and down on tramcars looking like law and order, yes, that was splendid . . . but one dreadful night all by myself, down Sydenham, I had to defend a letterbox. The trouble was the letterbox was red, you see. Aah, it's a red letterbox—it wasn't a Red Letter Day, it was just a damned cold night. Women came and stood around me and said "Boo, urrgh!" Menacing gestures, but they didn't hit me on the head with me armed as I was with me tin hat, all they did was boo and jeer. Menacing gestures there were, but no violence. "What are you doing?" "Get into the letterbox you silly little lout." "What are you? A bloody student? Get into the letterbox if you think you've got anything against us. Post yourself off anywhere!" This was not too bad, I wasn't very worried, but they were jeering and nasty, and women in a gang like that can do anything at all.

But I got away, there was no violence done to me. Yes, I'd have done violence back if any had been offered me, I would have done that because I've always been a mad fighting man. I mean that. But there was no violence. Then I got back to Canterbury College whereat I attended lectures and there I had my studies conducted by two very great Canterbury people, or one of them was, and the other wasn't. One was the great Professor Sinclair from Melbourne and the other was the great Doctor Helen Simpson, and it was these two people that brought me up. Professor Sinclair and Dr Helen Simpson. And what the hell did I know from Christ's bloody College except—you know—I was agin what *they* thought. But these people and the letterbox and the tramways strike made me begin to think, I had to ask myself why had they done this. I found that my two professors knew why, but I didn't. I'd gone in and simply because of the class structure had worn a band and a tin hat and a cudgel to knock down fellow New Zealanders. But what for? They weren't doing it for fun, nor their wives parading round the letterbox inviting me to get into it before they'd done me over. What for? At the end I came to think, it just crept on me, and Helen Simpson said at a tutorial well,you know, what would you do?

Now I said to Dr Helen Simpson, what would you do if they came—these louts—and broke your window in? She said I wouldn't do anything, I'd think. I would ask myself why? For what reason do they want to break my window? Yes Doctor, and I'd go away and I'd ask myself—cudgel, tin hat and armlet?—why? And I started to think, and there was a party at Bishop's Court that week and my gallant professor (I daresay Helen was there, I don't know), but my gallant, mad, radical, professor Sinclair was there and somebody said Do you know they've got out of hand?! And Freddy Sinclair from Melbourne roared his head off. He said Good, good, and My Lord Bishop, I hope they break your bloody windows in too! Well, all this was a bit hurtful for a little boy trying to think, just out of Christ's College and given a tin hat and a baton. Aha, you've got to learn to grow up. Mighty hard. I've always liked anything that was agin anybody, that's fine. But here are moral issues put against me for the first time. And the first thing I've got to do is thinking. Not too good. This is the Depression.

While watching the unemployed gather for a hunger march—they'd been on strike against the miserable provision, and they were in a state of semi-starvation—I heard the lean men cheer as they assembled. I knew of the hunger in the homes and as the men cheered, my eyes filled with tears. That was the night of the riots in Auckland. On the Saturday after the Auckland riots I was advertised to speak in the Auckland Domain. The government issued a notice prohibiting the meeting. Hundreds rang my home to ask would I be there and I decided that I had to go to keep faith with the people and keep them out of trouble. I'll never forget the occasion. As I walked along Karangahape Road towards Grafton Bridge thousands who had gathered to see what would happen walked behind Mrs Lee and myself as we moved onto the bridge the crowd filled the bridge from end to end. More gathered from the street leading to the bridge until Mrs Lee and myself were leading a mob of between eight and ten thousand people. As we came to the domain we found police at the gate and inside was a large detachment from the navy armed with small guns and a gatling gun. I had no intention of leading my following into trouble but of leading them away. I said to the sergeant of police at the gate: "We can't go in?"

"Try something," he challenged.

Unlike most policemen, he was militant. Most police, being workers, were in sympathy with the distressed thousands. I kept on walking and led the thousands around to a hill at the back of the enclosed domain and told my audience to sit down. And there we sat in thousands with a clear view of the armed forces in the domain. I set the thousands to singing. A person who was later tried for making a bomb and whom many later claimed was an *agent provocateur* urged an attack on the domain. "Don't be silly," I counselled, "just sit and sing." The Communist paper in its next issue assailed me for not leading the people against the law and the machine guns. I wasn't out to break the law, to challenge the police. The thousands already by just following and sitting down and singing had made an orderly protest. A sergeant came and asked me to send them home.

"I have your permission to speak?"

"Yes." He was a sensible man.

I told the thousands that they had made an orderly demonstration, that I wanted no violence of any sort, would they please disperse and go home peacefully, which they did, to the contempt of the *agent provocateur*. All MPs, apart from A.S. Richards, kept well out of the way.

A few days later Parry, Savage and myself visited the unemployed quarter of a relief camp at a hall on the North Road. Nothing explains more clearly the distress of the times and the readiness for militancy than the fact that the groups had hundreds of lengths of old galvanised piping cut into baton lengths for defense purposes should they be caught in a brawl. Our advice was to take the lot away and dump them, because in the wake of the two big riots we feared repressive measures against any suggestion of physical militancy. I think groups all over the city had similar armament.

My phone was tapped from the night of the riots and my friend Ormond Burton had a conversation over the phone. I remember how it went, or part of it:

"If we had the habits of a South American republic we could throw the government out this minute, but we prefer the democratic method. Just think what *could* have happened had the thousands outside the Town Hall walked a few yards to the Drill Shed and helped themselves to the rifles and ammunition."

Not that I was an advocate of any such action, I knew it would be doomed to failure. The following day the army moved the equipment from Rutland Street to Ngaruawahia, a wise move. I think it all stemmed from my phone conversation, listened to by a third person.

In the days following the riots, with all the Queen Street windows boarded up, business—already bad—plummeted to near bankruptcy. The big businessmen held a private meeting with the Auckland Labour MPs in the boardroom of the South British Insurance Company, a confluence of the Kelly Gang and Labour. All the Labour MPs spoke and the meeting agreed to make representations to the government for some easement in unemployed conditions. There was a subsequent slight improvement although the riots also caused the great separation of households, husbands from their wives and children, as workers were drafted to the slave camps, one of the cruellest acts of the government. That meeting in the boardroom, with blinds drawn, was never reported, and illustrates as much as any event the sense of crisis.

The night before the riots the unemployed had wanted to hold a great mass meeting in the Basin Reserve, but the authorities refused them. So they got permission from a private property owner to use a big vacant section somewhere up the back of Vivian Street, up Cuba Street way, and they were all peaceably having their meeting in there when without warning the police rushed them. They came charging through the gates, over the fences and belted hell out of them and grabbed one or two, and of course the crowd scattered. Well, that incensed the people of Wellington and that night they started to flock in the thousands. Cuba, Vivian and Manners Streets were just surging with people and the focal point was the corners of Vivian and Manners Streets. Many people who were there that night will well recall the scene—the thousands of people, and the specials—they had squads and squads, probably about 40 or 50 men in each, all standing, some facing one way running parallel with the footpath and facing the crowd on both sides—one facing the left footpath and one facing the next footpath and so on. And here also were thousands of people of all classes—you could see that—they weren't just unemployed or people out of work temporarily, you could see some of them could've come from any sort of home, well dressed, poor and the ragged-as-usual.

It would have been about seven o'clock at night when things really began to get hot; the special constables stood there and they weren't allowed to move and they took the most terrible tonguelashing from that crowd that I've ever heard. They were called everything on earth and insulted and taunted and some of them you could see the fear in their faces, and some of them were boiling with rage—they would've liked to have given it a go, but the crowd would have been too many for them. And as the time went on, about nine o'clock, you could feel the tempo rising and then the fire engines were sent up to further intimidate the crowd but the crowd still stayed back hurling these insults and taunts at the specials.

They'd kept the ordinary policemen off the street. The crowd were not incensed against the ordinary police, their hatred was directed against the specials. Some of the policemen were very decent chaps as I happen to know at the time and the general opinion was the police were OK except for that incident when they were ordered to charge the people holding the meeting in that vacant section—that is one case where they made a mistake. Well it got so hot by ten o'clock and it looked as if it was just going to break when the word came that the specials had to be marched right out of the streets of Wellington. They were told to right turn, quick march and then stomp, stomp, stomp. *Full retreat. But the roar of that crowd and the insults—I can still hear them to this day, I'll never forget them.*

Well this atmosphere continued for several days and everyone felt, if you spoke to any of them, that something's going to burst. You could feel it coming. And one day I was returning home up Clyde Quay and there was a big unemployed ike a scene from the Russian Revolution, the police ride into and break up a meeting held on private land at the top of 'uba Street, Wellington 1932. The following day rioting broke out in Lambton Quay and many windows were broken. Photo lexander Turnbull Library.

Photo Alexander Turnbull Library.

procession and they hoped to present a petition to the prime minister at parliament buildings. They wanted to march through the main streets of Wellington but they were forbidden. They had to come right up from Courtenay Place right along the wharf front at the back, and I happened to be going home to Island Bay at the time and I saw the head of this procession coming down from Courtenay Place and in the back street and I was rather amazed—as far as I could see there were old men, young men, women with kids, women with prams, all shapes and sizes, some of them well-dressed, some of them almost in rags and it stretched on and on. I really couldn't say how many were there but I do know this, that in reporting the riots the next day the newspapers said there were a few hundred participants in the procession. Well, it looked so impressive, I decided to go back so I followed along the street beside the procession and the chorus from the crowd "Come and join us, come and join us!" However, I kept on walking by them and they finally got down to parliament buildings.

Well the grounds were ringed with a solid cordon of police about three feet apart, right round. The procession halted there somewhere about perhaps two o'clock and thousands of people started to converge in that big wide area between the wooden parliament building and parliament building proper. As the afternoon wore on the crowd increased until it was just one great mass of people right up the side streets and everywhere. The leaders of the unemployed got up and gave speeches and said they were going to ask permission to enter parliament buildings and present the petition to the prime minister. But they were refused permission and there was an attempt to storm over the gates and I remember seeing the police push them back. This incensed the crowd.

The afternoon wore on. Even about four o'clock the street was so densely packed with people that the trams couldn't get through, so they stopped and trams were backed right up Lambton Quay and the other side down Thorndon way. The days were short then and just as it became dark, I was standing near the Cenotaph, hemmed in amongst the crowd, and only a few feet away there was a Hindu fruit barrow and a chap was standing there with one of the wooden-wheeled fruit barrows they used to push round those days and have a permanent standpoint, and I heard a voice cry out "Let's smash the bloody town up!" And with that, some of them rushed over, upended the poor old Hindu fruit barrow, oranges and bananas scattered all over the show and this was their first supply of ammunition and they picked them up. It looked to me to be about 30 or 40 men commenced the riot and I would say just about finished it too, the same group.

They started to bash the windows—they started to advance up Lambton Quay belting windows with oranges or bananas and as they broke the windows, particularly of hardware shops, they'd pick up spanners and iron bars and different gear like big tools and so on. And as they went up Lambton Quay you could hear the windows crashing, it was a horrible sound to hear. It was some feeling of horror and suspense, the crash of glass in the earholes and the thousands of people just out of curiosity probably, like most of us, and if you wanted to go against the crowd you just couldn't. They just surged right up behind these rioters, right up through the Quay.

Well, the police at parliament buildings tried to get through the crowd to get ahead of the rioters but they had no hope because a great mass had converged on Lambton Quay and as cars coming down Lambton Quay tried to break through the crowd, they'd grab the cars, occupants and all, and turn them upside down, their wheels spinning in the air. I passed several cars in the first few minutes on their hoods, scattered all over the Quay. And on it went—crash, crash, right up Lambton Quay and I was probably back about three chains or more, jammed in

Photo Alexander Turnbull Library.

A common sight during the nineteen-thirties. A delegation makes the pilgrimage up the steps of Parliament to demand of a minister that "the government do something". Photo Alexander Turnbull Library.

this crowd and you couldn't get out of it, and they were coming from side streets on the way up. I noticed ahead at Stewart Dawson's corner, corner of Willis Street and Lambton Quay, some mounted policemen on horses and they were trying to drive the crowd back but it was hopeless. I don't know where they scattered to—they just disappeared and on they went right up Willis Street, bashing every window. There were odd cases I believe where some of the business people had been sympathetic to the unemployed or had been good to some of them and evidently some of those people may have escaped but I remember it was well-known that one of them there made a special job of thanking them for past favours when some particular wrong had been done to the unemployed. From there they still progressed on, they couldn't stop them.

They'd brought specials, police reinforcements, rushed them in but they were surging onwards and they rounded Perrett's Corner and up that little short piece to Manners Street, but in front of the Royal Oak corner there was a solid mass of hundreds of specials and mounted policemen and ordinary policemen and I think that's where the crowd was finally defeated.

Well, the tramways strike. I don't really know the pros and cons of it, I wasn't a railwayman, but at that time they must've been going for better conditions naturally, or pay. They had a strike at a very bad time of course, it was in May 1932. I'd just arrived in town—no work, and I remember going down there and it was on the corner of Bealey and Fitzgerald Avenues at a big depot and you had to be there early. The first chap I met there, Johnny Porter, he was a member of the Communist Party at the time and he had a sugarbag full of rocks and they were going to stop the trams down there. There was Jim Andrews, he was on a bicycle, and the first tram was the Sumner tram that leaves early in the morning.

Unbeknown to us they had all these strikebreakers with tin hats called out from their business in town, there must've been twenty or thirty of them on the other side of the tram as it pulled out. And this scab motorman was instructed to go quietly, like they build up the tram and it can go slow, I think it's in series or something. Of course as soon as he poked his nose out there was a shower of rocks, everything went windows and all, and of course he panicked. He wrapped it up and dropped to the floor, ducked, and the tram picked up speed and shot off and uncovered all these bloody strikebreakers. It was a bit of a shock to the jokers. Of course they were all armed, batons, and they charged off then. We took to our scrapers, we had to from these damned hickory sticks and they knocked several down. I remember Selwyn Devereaux, he was knocked down—he was full of fight and they had to knock him up. Fellows grabbed him and took old Selwyn around the back. I found out later they even broke his jaw and he got three months' jail or something in Paparoa. It was winter time too, coming on May, June, July, August yes. I remember we all rushed up towards Ferry Road and I got away. I was barred on a bike with a chap and went rushing down. There was no show at all. One of these scabs came rushing out, tin hat and baton, and Jim Andrews on his bike rushed at him, took his foot off the pedal and bowled him. He got away too.

The strike went on, there was a silent demonstration and the Square was packed and Jock Matheson came round and addressed them. He said as much as if to say that if any women started anything in the Square, they would all be right behind us. So we marched to the Square and there was a woman laying down in front of one of the trams and I happened to turn round and see the policemen going for her. Anyway this woman was arrested and she got three months' jail. Incidentally she was pregnant at the time but they didn't make allowances for it.

Seamen demonstrate against wage cuts, Wellington waterfront January 1931, Fintan Patrick Walsh for once in the foreground. Photo Alexander Turnbull Library.

Even staid Dunedin contributed its share to the disturbances of 1932. Demonstrators gather in George Street in January and one local lawyer, alarmed at the evidence of unrest, took an axe to bed with him every night for the rest of the year. Photo Hocken Library.

The police immediately cordoned off a square in front of the GPO in the Square. They started diving in and diving out grabbing whoever they could and of course once you pulled back, they had you. They were rushing them up to the steps. I'll always remember this one chap, Percy Wigg, he's dead now, he sung out "To hell with Coates"—three months he got.

The reaction of the crowd was a silent demonstration, nobody spoke and it made the police very uneasy. The police were marching up and down but you could see they were very uneasy because of the silence of the demonstration. It had a great impact, I can remember that much. Nobody speaking at all and they just kept moving, you had to keep moving otherwise the police would have been in, but we kept moving, just step by step. The police had their instructions. I always remember Jack McKegley—he had a copy of the *Workers' Weekly* in his pocket—got an extra three months, six months in all he got.

If you look at my files you'll find there's a file there on the New Zealand Legion. The New Zealand Legion was led by a man called Dr Campbell Begg and he gathered together men of a professional nature, or people who were self-employed (not trade unionists and not businessmen so much as semi-professional people) and they formed organisations through New Zealand to advocate the running of New Zealand in a businesslike way, making the show work and having integrity, as they used to say, in politics. They had some aims which were pretty suspect when you came to look at them. They were a movement that could well have turned into a fascist movement if there had been enough demagogues at the top to organise them. But they remained a movement of the middle-class semi-professional, and didn't manage on the one hand to get a large following of workers, and on the other hand a big lot of capitalist backers because you've got to remember in New Zealand in those days a capitalist backer could only be a banker or insurance company or a merchant and they were supporters of the government anyhow and so this Legion (and they had one in Australia) didn't evolve into the kind of Mosleyite movement which was the fascist movement in Britain about the same time.

Just after the first war things were all right because we still had the advantage of wartime buying, but about 1921 they took a tumble. And at the same time they were trying to put returned servicemen on the land. No experience, they didn't have anything to guide them in it, there was no floor price for produce, no control of markets, no nothing, and these fellows had a pretty hard time of it all through the twenties. Things were just picking up for some of them in 1931 and suddenly the bottom just fell out of everything. A lot of us younger blokes could see that it was no go—the government just wasn't able to cope with it. Except for Coates. He was a man who knew what was what, a younger man, a returned man himself, and he could see what had to be done but he couldn't carry his party with him.

We young fellows left the Reform party and there was hell to pay, and some of us stood for parliament in 1931. We didn't win but we came pretty close to it. It was because of this discontent among the younger men that the Coalition was formed out of Liberal and Reform in 1931 because it was the only way for the party to survive and keep out the other lot. But that wasn't going far enough for us and when the election was over we set out to form the New Zealand Legion. It had a lot of support and it pulled a lot of influential people in behind it, but it started attracting older men as leaders and they wanted to regiment the whole thing. That was no good to us younger blokes because young people can't stand regimentation, so we got out.

Supporters of Mussolini attend a ceremony at the Wellington War Memorial in honour of a visiting Italian warship. Photo Alexander Turnbull Library.

Some people think it was a reaction to the 1932 riots, to the Unemployed Workers' Movement, things of that sort, and that a number of the supporters went Democrat in 1935. Well, they may have, I don't really know, but that wasn't what it was really all about. It was young men in the Reform Party who could see that the government just wasn't coping and they wanted to do something about it. There were other young men who felt the same way—Keith Holyoake was one—but they wouldn't leave the party. But we were young and impatient, impetuous in a way, and the Legion grew out of that.

The politicians of the day were completely baffled and impotent. George Forbes was the PM, quite unable to lead in any direction. His finance minister Downie Stewart kept the cashbox firmly locked, acting as he was directed by the banks. I think he said at one stage that if the Chairman of the Associated Banks were to come into his office and tell him to lie down on the floor while he ran up and down on him, he'd have to do it. That was when he resigned and Coates took over. There were, at the time, funds available, three millions in the Post Office building fund for instance, but no one dared to spend the money. There was, at one stage, a hunger march on Wellington from Gisborne, where the closing down of the railway works had left several hundred workers and their families high and dry. They said their piece and went home again. Nothing ever came of it. One morning I remember seeing an angry crowd milling round the entrance to parliament buildings. Some speakers tried to send them away, one in particular whose knees were knocking as he stood dangerously on top of a post. Nobody listened much and they finally lost patience and ran off up Lambton Quay, breaking windows as they went. It was a very ugly situation.

It must have been about the time that Dr Begg began to get worried. He issued an appeal for men of good will to rally around him, and rally around they did.

A membership figure that I recall being mentioned at one stage was 70,000; this after only a few months. There was a small magazine that I wrote for sometimes. There were meetings; a crowded Town Hall heard a very good address from Evan Parry, a well-known solicitor. There was a Dominion conference for the Legion, delegates coming from all over. One delegate was moved to remark that the country people could no longer support the towns in the manner to which they had become accustomed, and that was the general tone of the country delegates. Dr Begg had been afraid of the Communists but they were as confused and disorganised as anyone else, and I don't recall any evidence of their being a menace to anyone, or a help either. The name fascist was just beginning to be used, but its later implications were not then realised. I had joined because I was out of work and because I thought that things were in an awful mess and here seemed to be someone who was doing something. Dr Begg always impressed me as being very honest and sincere, not just looking for glory; he was an able man and a potential leader but quite non-political. There was a political vacuum there but he hadn't the experience or the desire to fill it. I think he despised politics and politicians. After the big conference the thing just seemed to fizzle out quietly and gradually. Dr Begg had rubbed the lamp and the genie had appeared but he had no orders to give it. Begg is reported to have said before he left for South Africa that only Labour had a policy. He left the leadership of the Legion to a Mr J.W. Andrews in Lower Hutt, but he didn't see himself as Mr Big in a dictatorship either, so that was the end of the Legion.

It was a period of slick nihilism. Nazi-ism was becoming of world-wide interest but we out here were mostly ignorant of it. Some of us were groping after the truth and trying to heal some of our wounds. Parochialism was rampant and many of us were convinced that it was fired by job holders. It's still the same today. Campbell Begg had been practising medicine in South Africa and I truly believe had become imbued with radical ideas. Not radical as to democratic theories but definitely anti-bureaucratic privilege. He wrote to some of us younger men here in Dunedin asking for our support in forming an organisation to counter the extension of local body government. This was his only plank. Groups had already been formed throughout New Zealand and it became clear that we were to receive bitter resistance and opposition, although we quickly had about 2,000 members locally. Where the name New Zealand Legion came from I have no idea but I suspect that Begg was inspired by German and South African ideologies. It was remarkable, support came from all sorts of unexpected quarters. In Dunedin we progressed so quickly that Begg offered to come down and address a public meeting. His brother, James Begg, another doctor, pooh-poohed the whole setup and pressed us to stop.

Begg arrived and we, the committee, had a number of meetings with him. His purposes were vague and we presumed he was holding off for the big public meeting we had organised in the Town Hall with a seating capacity of about 4,000. I was the Otago branch chairman so I took the chair. Knowing so little of what Begg had in his mind, my introduction was very brief and I handed over to him. Gradually it became apparent that he envisaged a new political party to contest the elections. He wandered on interminably and his audience became restless. He leaned down to me and asked if he had said enough and I replied quite bluntly: "Too much." He had spoken for one and a half hours and told us nothing. Afterwards we met in a tearoom and when he asked us what we thought it was obvious to us all that he'd struck a death blow. We all resigned. Quite frankly, we all understood that the Legion was to combat the growing multiplicity of local bodies of all types and the burden of taxation created by those bodies. Quite a few of our supporters threw in their lot with the Democrats in 1935.

If you were ill, you couldn't go to a hospital unless you went through a whole rigmarole of how much money have you got and do you keep a canary—because there were no free hospitals and no free doctors and the number of people who died from pneumonia or even died of starvation was quite considerable. I know it hasn't been mentioned much, but I know of people who died from lack of food in the Depression, older people. And of course the incidence of disease increased tremendously. But one of the interesting things about the Depression was there was not any thieving or burglaring along the lines that you get today, when you have young people unemployed. Today you have young people who have come from a generation where there have been jobs and for some reason or other, a lot of pinching and thieving is going on. Now this wasn't characteristic of the Depression. What was characteristic was that the people kept on keeping on with these terrible conditions; agitating, talking, standing on deputations, waiting in queues, until finally, as a group, as a society, they could stand it no longer. I remember the women at Dunedin lying on the tramlines in final desperation as a gesture against authority and then the riots breaking out in all the centres. This was the explosion of people who could no longer stand the terrible strain on their social inheritance. They just burst forth in uncontrolled anger just to smash . . . it wasn't a matter of hooliganism or criminality, it was the revolt of the people.

Making Do

I used to get things spinning,
I used to dress like a lord,
mostly I came out winning,
but all that's gone by the board;
my pants have lost their creases,
I've fallen down on my luck,
the world has dropped to pieces
everything's come unstuck.

Roaming the cliffs in the morning light,
hearing the gulls that cry there,
not knowing where I'll sleep tonight,
not much caring either,
wandering above a sea of glass
in the soft April weather,
wandering through the yellow grass
close to the end of my tether.

A.R.D. Fairburn

One saw in the newspapers about the decline in dairy prices and the export trade in produce and this sort of thing, but I think the first time that the Depression really struck me was in April 1932 on the occasion of the riots. The first riot was on Thursday night and on Friday morning at school we talked about it extensively. It was of course *the* subject—the fact that the navy came over in a contingent and marched in Queen Street, the fact of the special constables being gathered up and being sworn in and issued with arm bands and waddies—this sort of thing. The feeling of apprehension that went through our community. There is one good memory that I have. I was a cadet CSM at school and we had our cadet uniforms and on the morning of Friday 10 April a van drew up at the door of our school and several senior boys were summoned from their classes and we were told to get in the van and we did, and inside it were several instructors of the Defence Department, in uniform. We were told that we were going to the Kingsland drill hall and we went down there and we systematically took the bolts out of all the 22 rifles and 303s and we gathered all these together and put them into the back of the van and so we disarmed all of the firearms that could be found. This was the most vivid early memory I have, although I can remember in class that day too, talking about the enormity of the situation when servicemen had to be called out in uniform and marched through town in bunches. Then of course the big riot came on Friday night and I missed all of this because I was a

Photo Alexander Turnbull Library.

ıg the Farrow marchers. The Gisborne unemployed were probably the best organised in New Zealand. After a successful week ɜmonstrations in Gisborne they prepare to march to Wellington to dramatise their despair. On the way they were met with offers ɔffee from farmers and the army with machine guns in Palmerston North. Photo Max Riske.

ɔ Max Riske.

schoolboy and I didn't know that it was going to occur on Friday. But I can remember the disorder on Saturday in Queen Street and this was quite heart-breaking.

I was born in 1908, war broke out in 1914, I was only about six. War finished round about 1918-19, I was just a kid. So anyway when the Depression was approaching I was listening to my mother and father who said: go and see the world. I was just telling my good lady this afternoon how a fellow named Trilby Adams (we went to school together), bought an old 1918 Ford and he said "C'mon, we'll get away and get a job." So we did. We went away and got a job. When we got to a place called Karamea he said "I've got an uncle here, he'll look after us." But they couldn't afford to keep us so I said "We'll nick into Stratford." Anyway Trilby's uncle said "What're you going to do now?" I said "We'll go into the Public Works and get a job." So we walked into the Public Works office and got a job. We had a ticket to go way back in the back country, Kiori—mud up to your ruddy neck. And his car! He was worried about his car. So I said "Forgit about yer car, we'll walk up." We had a ticket to get a job. Up we go and you couldn't knock on a tent door so I just went in, there was a light there and I said "Is your name Bert Henry?" He says "That's right." I said "We've just come in." He says "There's your tent." So we slept in that tent that night, then Trilby went home, and I stayed. And I had some great times.

Bert Henry, he came from the Coast, he was a great mate of Harry Holland. Bert Henry was a real man. He took a shine to me, I don't know why he did, but I liked him. I liked him for what he was, I thought he was real. He was old enough to be me granddad. He had three sons and one daughter. He lost a son off the Westport wharf, drowned. Then the 'flu epidemic came, lost his wife, lost another son and the doctor bloke said you gotta go, you gotta get away and relax. So he went away and he got himself an 8 x 10 tent up in the ruddy scrub and he was my best friend. And we were both in the public works together. Yeah, Public Works and I was only a teenager, and I liked him, I liked him because for what he was.

So anyway, I'll never forget you know, my camp was about a mile from the Hargoods camp and old Bert Henry knew damned well that I used to pass that camp. And I used to nick in to see if this home brew was . . . you know when the froth comes up . . . and the Hargoods asked if I could skim it while they were away. Well I used to nick in and skim it you know. I never infringed on another man's camp without permission. Anyway I used to skim this with me hand, I'd skim the froth off and see she was workin'. I knew the trouble—they'd be drunk for a month, but that wasn't the point. So anyway, I'm up there working, down below their tent, and Henry goes by. "Where are the Hargoods?" he says. "I says "They're not at home." "You know what," he said to me—"The buggers are in Stratford on the booze." "Well," I said, "Bert, they could be." "Well I'll go up and salt their grog." And he did. He went into that camp, a six-man tent and I've always held that agin old Bert. Salted their grog. In those days, a man never went into a tent unless you was invited. And he went in and picked up a couple of pound in a paper bag or somethin and salted their grog. I says "Bert, you'd be looking for trouble. You done wrong Bert." He says "Bugger 'em," he says. "They're going to come back to work."

Well when they went back to the tent and they're drinking up their bloody pea soup you know, it was like pea soup—"Some bugger's salted me beer." I said "Hargood it wasn't me." "Who was it?" he says. I wouldn't split if it was Bert Henry, dinkum, I wouldn't split. They were the days when a man was a man. No, I met some great blokes those days. I was only young but it was the greatest education I ever had. Truly.

ɪy people thought that if only people could be encouraged to get things moving again the Depression would be over almost ight away. One of the ideas mooted was the employment of unemployed youth. A procession on behalf of the Youth Employment ɪpaign passes down High Street Christchurch and into oblivion. Photo Auckland Weekly News.

My wedding dress was bought from a secondhand shop and all our clothes came from a secondhand shop. My sister and I used to mend our own shoes. If we wanted to go to a dance we'd have to mend our own shoes. We'd just have enough to get in with, no extra, just the shilling.

My father worked at the railways goods sheds, and he came home one day with a truck full of cabbages, they were to be dumped, and we got sacks full of them and all the neighbours that we could find came with their sacks and filled their sacks, rather than dump them. He said that there was a lot of that going on, food being dumped instead of giving it to the people.

The Sanitarium down the road here—Weetbix—you could get broken Weetbix, about half a sugarbag full for two bob. And as a matter of fact, as you know, they are some sort of a religion, Seventh Day Adventists,. . . yes that's right. They had chaps going round, a woman and chap really, and that was the staple diet that they offered to you—all that. Weetbix and a bit of Marmite and things like that. Had that kind of thing during the Depression. Staples were bread, brains and there was tea that was dirt cheap but nobody had any money. Bread, Marmite, Weetbix, there wasn't too much meat. I used to bike out to the freezing works and get a forequarter for about 2/6 or something.

I remember one incident, we were in a place—6/- a week board we paid, it was a house with two rooms. I must have been washing this day and bending over the washing basket I had, and a couple of days later I went back to the basket and I found a shilling in the basket. So my husband biked off and he got six pennyworth of coal, fourpence worth of fish and chips and a threepenny cabbage. And we ate that night. We had a fire and we had some fish and chips and cabbage. Even to find a shilling was something worthwhile then.

They had community singing in the Trades Hall and people would go along and sing their heads off. They had it in the Civic Theatre too, in the Trades Hall to begin with and then they went to the Civic Theatre. In my opinion I think that was only a gimmick to get you away from the right track. All that singing,. . . I never went to it, I had nothing to sing about. But they used to have all these gimmicks. They used to bring in these songs, "We're In The Money" and "Happy Days Are Here Again" and no bugger was happy and nobody had a feather to fly with. You know, all the gimmicks were there. They organised what have you. But they never organised anything that would alleviate the conditions of the unemployed and there were some terrible conditions. I remember one chap in particular at North Beach, if ever it had come up a northwester I think the house would've gone. I think he sawed every other 4 x 2 up in the roof to put on the fire. He didn't have anything. It was all very well, oh chaps would come and say "Oh there's a farmer, he's got so many head of sheep he can't handle it." But how the hell are you going to get there to get it? And "There's plenty of wood at so and so", but we had no chance to get it. People didn't think of that. They used to put that in the paper, this, that, and the next thing. But you'd no way of getting it. A lot of that went on.

I went through the Depression years rather easily because under the advice of a friend of mine I bought some land in Stokes Valley, 2½ acres of land for two hundred and fifty pounds. On it we built a bach and three other girls and I lived there. One girl and I, we got little jobs working half a day and I earned 15/- a week, she earned 10/-. That was for a couple of years. I had a vegetable garden and we had a half acre of bush on this section and I used to cut down ti tree for firewood to allow others to grow, so that it wasn't destroyed.

Student teachers entertain the children of relief workers to a Christmas treat. Games were played in front of the college, and Father Christmas, in traditional garb, distributed sweets. Photo Auckland Weekly News.

They made their own fun in the Depression. Photo Alexander Turnbull Library.

So with our vegetables and the little money we earned, we got along very well really, and we had nobody to keep up with because more or less everybody, even the employed, were in the same boat. When I learned I could get assistance from the Hutt, I used to cycle in once a week and got this 3/- worth of supplies which consisted of condensed milk, candles, butter and tea. One couldn't get other than those things.

Shall I tell you about the little joke? Well, one day the shopkeeper who happened to have a big store at the DIC corner it was called then, he said to me "Have you come to spend ten pounds?" and I said "When I have ten pounds to spend I'll buy something I don't want." He said why? I said "I have to watch every twopence to see if I'm spending it wisely before I dare spend it, and it would be a relief to have ten pounds to throw away." So then he said that that explained to him why poor people who inherited fortunes squandered it all away. So from then on he became friendly and allowed me to have prunes and raisins and dates, anything but tinned milk and candles.

I think a lot of unemployed reached a stage of liking their unemployment. They weren't tied for so many hours a day and it was a free life providing you could get enough to eat. And I struck it lucky under those conditions. But then later I went to Wellington, somebody asked me to go, and I managed the International Bookshop. And there I noticed everybody used to buy pies and dry sandwiches and all this sort of thing and I thought that wasn't any good, so I organised lunch for quite a few people and everyone paid into the kitty 1/6d a week and I provided a meal for threepence a day, and any visitor had to pay fourpence for the meal. I used to buy tomatoes—which were cheap, dried beans or spaghetti and things like that, and make the meal at home, then reheat it. We could supply everybody with a decent lunch. It was better than stale pies and stale bread.

That's when I met my friend Mrs Baker and used to go to her place for lunch the day I collected my three shillings' worth of rations. And she gave me a shilling to go and buy something for lunch which I thought was very extravagant—a whole shilling to spend on lunch. So it gives an idea of the value of money. You could buy quite a bit with a shilling. Butter was 1/6d a pound and lambs fry was 3d a pound or sometimes you'd get those things for nothing—the butcher would give away offal and if you bought soup bones, well they were not bones, they had meat on so people could have a stew out of soup bones, which you don't get today. And I think there was a sort of feeling of helpfulness amongst people. You didn't seem to be envious of people.

One thing I remember was when people started working again, after the Labour government came in, we didn't see anybody for several weeks because everybody was too tired—they used to go to bed when they finished work, they hadn't worked for years and they had to get conditioned to working consecutive hours, and it was very noticeable that it took quite a few weeks for people to get adjusted to working.

It was surprising what you could live on, like you used a lot of dried beans and dried peas and it was surprising, with a few tomatoes which you could probably get for about 2d or 3d a pound, you could make a big meal. And with bread, and butter was 1/6d a pound (it stayed that price for years, I think right through the war it stayed at that price, it's only in recent years that the price of buter's gone up). People used to collect food in sugarbags, the idea of the sugarbag . . . it was a receptacle to put things in, and that was the great thing about a sugarbag. They would carry them, if they didn't have a proper bag well that's the next best thing. And then of course sugar was always sold in those, I don't think it's sold that way now.

'any, particularly those in work, thought that Depressions were caused by a lack of confidence and sought to end the hard times y cheering everyone up. During Prosperity Week in Wellington 1933, a decorated float passes the band rotunda in Oriental Bay. Not 'ctured is the "Unemployment Queen" entered in the procession by the relief workers and made entirely of bits of wire. The city thers were not amused by this intrusion of bitterness and reality into their ineffective play acting. Photo Alexander Turnbull Library.

In the depths of the Depression they had a "cheer up" week in Wellington. Oh, it was a *sad* affair. The fire brigade went around to Oriental Bay at night and played their hoses on the water, and the Electricity Department shone coloured search-lights on the water. Then they had dancing in Oriental Parade. They used to have community singing in the Town Hall at lunch-time too. The idea was if you could get people to forget their troubles and regain their confidence, then the Depression would just disappear. I don't think it worked.

Oh yes—they had a queen carnival in association with it too. This that and the other organisation entered their competitor, and the unemployed entered their 'unemployment queen'. She was made entirely of wire. There was hell to pay and I think someone ended up in court about it. Disturbing the peace or something. I don't know what came of it.

An unemployed demonstrator gets his "come-uppance" at the state opening of parliament 1934. Policemen nurse bruised fingers. Photo Jack Locke.

I remember lots of those blokes on the wharf, who were on relief and quite a lot of them were agitators who were involved in unemployed workers' movements and this sort of thing, but most of what I got out of them, being more specialised, concerned with their political activities, their running away from policemen. One of them told Bill O'Reilly, the waterfront poet, of an extraordinary experience—of climbing up on a certain statue and waving a red flag or something in the middle of one of the unemployed demonstrations, and the police trying to climb up to him and he going round and round this certain statue treading on their fingers. He regarded this as the sort of highlight of his defiance of authority in the case of the Depression.

I think he spent a lot of time sending up authority during his trial. He was tried for the usual thing, which was mischief or being a public nuisance or disorderly behaviour. During his trial he insisted on defending himself and taking notes, and he bought an enormous pencil, it had a six inch diameter, that he'd bought at Woolworths—one of those trick things that you sold for the kids to fill their Christmas stockings with—and he used this and a tiny wee notebook. The pencil could only write one letter on a page and taking his notes on this caused all sorts of guffaws in the courtroom and generally sent up the whole proceeding. When he got to Mount Crawford prison—I think he was given two weeks—he insisted on being treated as a political prisoner and being put apart from the criminals. He said he wasn't a criminal and he stood on his dignity. The great thing about this is its festive atmosphere. He obviously regarded this as a sort of enjoyable experience and not something terribly sad.

Housing: Depression style. A relief worker entertains visitors while sharpening his knife (for Adam Hamilton, Minister of Unemployment?). Photo NZ Herald.

I was 21 in 1931 and I was working on a bridgebuilding project and studying engineering by correspondence. I'd bought a bit of cut-over white pine swampland over near Otorohanga, about 33 acres, and then there were suddenly no more jobs of any sort for single men like myself. One day a fortnight at seven and six if the local body felt like it but I was told that as I owned land I didn't qualify for it, so I built a shack on my land which was a mass of white pine stumps overgrown with giant blackberry and one or two very large yellow pines which were not what the millers wanted when they cut the rest. These I felled and then cut into sections for battens. The trees were so large that working a crosscut saw by myself to cut through took up to seven thousand strokes. Then I split the battens and carried them out on my shoulders through the swamp and blackberry, getting large gall sores on my shoulders in the process. I tried to sell them at seven and six a hundred. People would buy them but couldn't pay for them. Still, I persevered and somehow or other I existed until things righted themselves again.

Scrim

I was transferred to Auckland at the end of 1932—it was a temporary transfer—and up there, having been somewhat awakened by my Wellington experience, the situation was worse. This was about the time that Scrim and his Friendly Roads radio station was making all kinds of motions to government that farmers would offer meat but the Railways wouldn't cart it and therefore people in towns couldn't get it. I think listening to the Friendly Roads station was possibly my first leaning towards the Labour type of outlook. On Sunday evenings you could walk along the street and hear the radio sets going in all the houses and everyone listened to the Friendly Roads station when Scrim was on the air.

He used to play a few hymns or popular songs and talk to people about social justice in general. He frequently had other people coming and doing a lecture. I've forgotten exactly how long it ran but I think it could have been 9 until 10, something of that sort. But he had this tremendous following and mainly because he was saying the human things. In and around about under the Grafton Bridge you could go any night of the week and find people sleeping out under newspapers because they had nowhere to go and no food to eat. The most distressing thing I think was that in some of the churches in some of the areas the people refused to have destitute people in, even to sleep in their places, you know, they had nice carpets on the floor and this somewhat added to my views that this was wrong and since that I've had a sort of a Labour leaning, leaning towards human beings rather than towards profits.

Scrim appealed to the ordinary bloke in the street and gave him some sort of hope. He said things about the Establishment—if you like—that nobody else was game to say, the newspapers certainly weren't saying. He did offer them a popular, down-to-earth brand of religion, and he did do a lot of good work in sort of getting money in and handing it out. He did work in conjunction with the City Missioners, people like that. And the whole point was that there was somebody talking in their own words to the people who were going through a hell of a time and couldn't see any end to it. It was just as simple as that. Just in the same way as Winston Churchill appealed during the war years—he talked language that the people understood.

Rev. C.G. Scrimgeour (left) and friend, city missioners in Auckland, set out "to see for themselves" in the garb of the unemployed. What they saw shocked them profoundly. Photo C.G. Scrimgeour.

It wasn't actually called a Depression in 1927 but it was obvious that something very serious was happening because the whole purpose of my coming to the job I was in was to inaugurate social service work for the Methodist Church. And at that period of time it was obvious—to the discerning people anyhow—that there was some need for someone and so they invited me to come down and begin their efforts which involved a lot of things that had nothing to do with, say, the Depression, but they had a lot to do with social problems.

The main thing I think was that they were conscious of the fact that no serious attempt was being made by the church and while there were plenty of do-gooders (there were very admirable people who were always on the job doing good), there was something lacking. And when I came to Auckland (by the way it was the first time I had been in a city and I knew nothing at all about social work—I knew a hell of a lot about poverty because I was born in it and brought up in it) and so I thought that the best thing I could do was to go and have a look. So I left my shaving for two or three days and got some old clothes—they used to be very fond of old-clothes drives in those days so there was no shortage of old clothes in any church organisation—and I got a fellow from the Theological College to keep me company. We both dressed up and we went out and we spent three days wandering around, finding out not from social workers and not from churches, but from the people who were involved—these were the down and outs, and people who generally wouldn't talk to anybody. But when you were in disguise they talked to you and they told you exactly what the situation was.

It became obvious that not only was the charity work a complete and absolutely archaic thing (that is, the church believed that the poor have always been with you kind of philosophy) and these things were do-gooder operations. The only claim I can make to this was that I did not like the do-gooders. I remember the Charitable Aid Board that my mother had gone to, where she got 2/6 a week to help keep the family of six and so charity to me was not twice blessed as the church people said but twice cursed. And I made it quite clear that it was my view that the operations had got to be a totally different kind of operation.

We had in the Methodist organisation a thing called the Down and Outs Mission. The main purpose of the Down and Outs Mission was to feed people who were chronic alcoholics and were indeed people who were down and out, not through poverty, not through unemployment, they were just hopeless cases. To feed them we relied upon the weather, because the pie-maker who made the pies for Ellerslie Racecourse and had the contract for selling pies, was a fellow who, if the weather was bad, he didn't sell his pies so he would then send his carriers in and the pies were dumped on the steps of an old church in Airdale Street, these crates and crates of pies. Then the down and outs all came up and they were given pies.

So there were all the organisations that did this kind of work called social work and while it would be unkind to belittle it, it was nothing to do with the problems that were later to arise as the Depression became more obvious. The Depression started to become obvious when people became unemployed, and the unemployed figures rose alarmingly and very soon it was obvious that what had happened in Wall Street and the general world-wide Depression, was beginning to make itself felt in New Zealand.

Now the reason that the change of pattern came into my type of work was that I took the part of the unemployed. These people were victims, they were not perpetrators of pauperism or scroungers, they were people who were just honestly short of food. And I very quickly realised that this was purely false.

There was no such thing as a shortage of food. There was no such thing as a shortage of people who could build houses. There was no such thing as a shortage of wool. My reasoning as a young social worker was that there are only three needs that people have—food, clothing, and shelter. Now then in New Zealand, although there might have been a monetary crisis, there was no reason whatever for there to be a shortage in any of these three basic essentials. But this did not please the authorities, it didn't even please the church authorities, and it certainly didn't please the political authorities, because I said "This is all unnecessary".

The farmers were prepared to give their beef away so I started a chain of butcher shops and the Farmers' Union organised the slaughter of cattle in the freezing works at Waikato and they said you can have the meat providing we have the offal. By this time there were tens of thousands unemployed. The Minister of Unemployment was also the Minister of Railways. So I went to see him (Adam Hamilton) and I led a delegation of these nice social working people to see him at the Post Office in Auckland and I advanced this argument that we can get all the meat we want, so I want the right to draw back enough butchers, I can get all the shops I want—because by this time businesses were feeling the pinch and shops were closing down all over the place so there was no difficulty in getting shops. So I got shops. Then the Minister of Unemployment could not, as the Minister of Railways, grant us free transport from Waikato to Auckland for the meat that had been donated by the farmers. Farmers couldn't sell it. So I was a little concerned about it and I spoke on behalf of all those people who were with me—all good people—and he said no, that we can't do that because the Railways are already losing money and we have a responsibility to the bond holders. Now, I was not an economist, and I had not been trained in these things at all, but this made me angry and so I said to him that—"Mr Hamilton, what about your responsibility to your own people in New Zealand—to feed them? You are the government. What about that responsibility? Let's forget about the bond holders for the time being." And Adam Hamilton said "This is an outrageous suggestion. This is a suggestion of repudiation, horrifying in tone." So I said "Well, it's a repudiation of either the bond holders or the people who need food," and it became rather an unpleasant debate in which he got extremely angry (I was angry all the time but I didn't show it) and so he said the interview was over. I got up and I thought all the social workers—because I was Secretary of the Social Workers' Association and they all knew what I said was correct—I thought they'd all come with me. Instead of that, not one came and I walked out on my own, and then Adam Hamilton went into a nice kind of Presbyterianised, Calvinistic dialogue about his background and his Christian ethics and so on, and succeeded in convincing the social workers that these ideas were all very well but they were not ethical and they were certainly not sound or Christian.

So the next step—the meat scheme—went ahead. I opened the butcher shop and paid the 10/- or whatever it was (we had to pay a certain amount to get the meat up, 10/- a side I think it was) and we opened up the butcher shop with unemployed butchers who got their unemployed pay, nothing more, they didn't get butchers' wages. They brought their own tools and so we opened up at least five butcher shops directly we could guarantee a bit of meat. The farmers' organisation, the Farmers' Union, was entirely responsible for organising the meat.

The part of the New Testament that appealed to me was that Christ was a social crusader who took a whip and drove the money-changers out of the temples, and this was my background that reacted immediately to Adam Hamilton's thoughts of looking after the bond holders. So the meat thing went ahead very well, and then I decided that the next thing was boots. Boots were essential because everybody had worn their sandshoes out. These fellows who went into the country to work for their 10/- a week were working in sandshoes and they didn't last very long. So I said, well, there are plenty of old boots because in our clothes drives we get lots of boots, but they all needed repairs because they were throwouts. And so I went and enquired of two or three bootmakers and they said there was plenty of leather, no shortage of leather. So I said "Well, if I got the bootmakers, would you give us some leather?" And they said they couldn't give it to us but could sell it to us for what they bought it for. So we started up a series of boot repair shops. You could go in, sometimes even the unemployed bootmakers who were working there had to split the leather to make it go a bit further. But they at least shod people reasonably well. This again attracted a great deal of animosity. One of the leading social workers said that this was taking bread out of the mouths of the bootmakers. I said "But all these fellows are bootmakers." The fellows who were working were bootmakers and the only people who were losing anything were the people who had sold us the leather at less than the commercial price. So the boot depots went on.

We were also gathering clothing, there was shoe leather being provided and there was meat, which was the main protein necessary and then they got in addition to that part of the social work effort I had organised, enabled me to give a 5/- grocery order each week to each family. Didn't matter how many there were, that was all the money there was, so this was the social work effort. And when this became quite a noticeable thing that there was a difference—there was a social responsibility that had nothing to do with the love of God or the mercy of God, it had something to do with the conditions under which ordinary New Zealanders were living which I understood perfectly well. You'd find out that there was a shop that wasn't there any more, it might've been a dairy, it might've been a chemist shop, it would be something that wasn't there and someone would say oh, he went broke. The bankruptcy notices were always read with great care and they were always published in the papers so they got pretty full reportage by official Court advertising, and this gave the indication. But most people felt it because they themselves couldn't escape. The businessman couldn't escape—he was in a hell of a position because his revenue started to fall and so then he began to feel the pinch and he was always a good mark for me because I'd go in and probably get a donation of fifty pounds from a fellow who couldn't really afford fifty pounds but he was willing to try and help because he would say unless we do something about this we'll all go broke. So it wasn't the psychology of the workers only, it was the psychology of the businessmen that carried this thing on to a much more definite level of conscious appreciation of what it meant.

Things got very rundown just before the 1935 thing. First of all the clothing was very bad and the old clothes drives started to disappear because there were no old clothes—people were wearing them. The obvious thing was, if you saw a photograph of a crowd, you could tell that those people were suffering. I think malnutrition was the one that was least obvious and probably the most important because then you began to get illness, and that illness wasn't a visible illness, it wasn't a contagious disease, and consequently there were people who were literally dying on their feet. There was no free medical treatment, in any case no free medical treatment would have been any good—they had to be fed. And the charity which was in force was so paltry—this idea of Charitable Aid Boards, you know, you want to go through the history, they were the most horrifying attack on problems that related to people. Charitable Aid Boards were the stigma of everybody who went to them, and were anyhow

Repairing second hand boots became a fulltime occupation for some out of work bootmakers. The men on relief work needed the boots and the bootmakers needed the work. In Auckland Uncle Scrim's mission begged leather from the suppliers at cost and set up a chain of boot repair centres, often using the premises previously occupied by bankrupt businesses, and often too splitting the leather to make it go further. Photo Alexander Turnbull Library.

The Rev. A. Armstrong and some of the relief workers repairing boots and shoes for the Central Relief Depot at Seatoun, Wellington 1931. Photo NZ Free Lance.

useless, because they didn't get enough. There wasn't much opportunity for any dignity about it because you took a billy, or you could go to a biscuit factory for that matter and you could gather up the chips of broken biscuits. These fellows were most generous, you could get them at sixpence a shovelful of broken biscuits at some of the big biscuit factories. There was nothing dignified about this, there was nothing you could say was very terrible about it except that the kids all enjoyed a little bit of sweetness. The soup kitchens were just a matter of taking along a mug if you were a down and outer, or a jam tin or anything else and then a ladle of soup was put into it. It was as simple as that. It wasn't a very dignified occupation for the people who dished it out either. It was nothing like the Meals on Wheels of today's social efforts.

The variety of rackets that people got up to was very often emphasised. I had to deal with a good deal of this myself because people would become alive to all the tricks of the trade—after all they had to to keep alive—and other people got angry about it. I just simply set about forming up an organisation where there was a central clearing house so that everybody got their fair share and not just the clever ones who went round and got stuff and sold it. One of the favourite occupations of the unemployed was that if a fellow was being sent away to the country, they would ask him where he was going to, and he would say he was going, say, to Te Kuiti. "Oh, when you get there, look here's 9d," (you could send a telegram for 9d). "Please send me this telegram." And they would write it out for him. "Job here waiting bring boots and packs" or "Bring boots and slash hooks" or "Bring boots and tent". Then of course this fellow goes into a businessman and he was shown the telegram and he would probably get his fare. This kind of thing was always generally faked and Businessmen's Relief Service, which was part and parcel of my combined operation with all the charities, was to simply stop this so that when a businessman gave something he knew he was giving it to a genuine cause. But it was pretty desperate.

There were quite a lot of people who begged for 3d to have a drink, because if you had 3d to buy a drink, you could then go and have a bit of counter lunch. You got a piece of cheese and a beer—for a man that was a pretty good meal for the middle of the day when they had nothing at home. Unfortunately it wasn't something you could take home to the wife and kids. But begging on the street was an extremely rare thing.

It was harder on women than on anyone else of course. That was why I insisted that when orders were handed out for groceries, that it was made out in the wife's name, because there were quite a lot of fellows who would go and trade on these coupons. I've seen a grocery order on Hutchesons, the storekeepers, and while I'd no objection to seeing on a return docket sometimes a packet of cigarettes (which weren't quite as dear as they are now), if I found that there was not food for the family as well, I would then make the order out to the wife only and put 'No one else' on the bottom of it. Then she could go down and get her groceries. The orders were practically all basic. You would find that flour, sugar, butter and—strangely enough—aspirin. And a box of matches, not a packet, a box of matches. Sometimes a tin of golden syrup. You got sort of to know this. You knew that no, you can't object to people having a little bit of sweetness. Other than that it was just simply the ordinary, very low-priced articles. And I will say this for Hutchesons, they always managed to knock a little bit off the price. Golden syrup was a luxury. It appeared, but you didn't growl about it because it didn't appear very often. Generally people had an absolutely impossible diet. That's why the toll on health was so severe—it was purely nutrition. Then people became accustomed to this and they didn't know what nutrition was any more. You couldn't buy fresh vegetables if you lived in the city. If you lived a little bit out you could grow a few, but you couldn't buy them. You couldn't buy fruit although it was falling down off the trees by the hundreds of tons; there was no means of getting it in. The nutritional thing didn't throw itself up for some time. Then it became pretty obvious that the dental caries and all this sort of thing were nutritional disorders. During the Depression of course too, the doctors were almost as badly off as their patients; the doctors were magnificent people. They tried to do everything—but it's no good writing out a prescription if you can't go to the chemist. So they had to just try and suggest ways and means. If a child had scabs or sores or something, they would try and give a little bit of cheap ointment. But the Auckland doctors were magnificent people. I never had one refuse ever to see someone who was sick, and sometimes they were desperately sick. But then the doctors had a problem. What do you do? You see malnutrition in an acute form, but what do you do about it?

It got so in the end there was bound to be trouble—and there was trouble. The postal workers were having a meeting in the town hall, it wasn't the unemployed. But the unemployed decided to support the postal workers, so they marched up under the leadership of a fellow called Jim Edwards to support the postal workers. When they got the the Town Hall they found that the doors were shut and the police were there in force (very unusual force by the way because the police were becoming alerted and aware that this was now becoming a dangerous situation) so the police tried to tell the unemployed to go away and the unemployed didn't go away.

The whole thing started accidentally and the smashing raids started. (By the way the unemployed used the battens off my church fence, which I'm always proud of.) It all happened because a sergeant of police who knew Jim Edwards quite well went down and said to him "Jim, stand up and tell these boys that the hall is *full.*" Well, Jim Edwards walked up the side of the street, and the policemen didn't want to be seen with him otherwise that would have been giving the show away, so Jim Edwards forces his way up to the edges of the Town Hall and the sergeant just walked round the other side. But the sergeant hadn't been able to tell his police force that Jim Edwards was coming to tell them to go home and Jim Edwards walked into this semi-circle of police, put up his hands to say "I'm telling you the town hall is *full* and they're not stopping you because you're unemployed. Go home." At that moment a young policeman hit him across the head and tore his scalp and he had 37 stitches put in it, so it was a pretty hard blow. Once the blood started to flow that crowd simply went mad and the first things they could find were the churches of the Airdale Street Mission. So they ripped the fence down and with those palings they smashed the windows. This rioting brought into focus a new problem that wasn't the problem of charity meeting a need, it was a social problem which had to be tackled in a totally different way, by some other method. The next morning after the riots (and this was what caused all my trouble in later years with broadcasting) was that I went on the air and said that these people were just people who were mistaken in their methods, but they were desperate people, and they did not set off to create a riot, but if the battens that they used are effective in drawing the attention of the government and the people of New Zealand to an unnecessary situation, then that's the best use the Methodist Church has been put to in the last hundred years. Of course the newspapers were all screaming in black headlines and the Methodists didn't like what I said at all. But the important thing was that it marked the changing of emphasis from charity to social and political responsibility. I kept on that line, I didn't stop there at all. I said "There is a world crisis, all right, Mr Hamilton has told us there's a world crisis, we know there's a world crisis, but we in New Zealand are fortunate to live in a country which has an abundance of food. At Henderson, today, there are hundreds of tons of apples rotting because it doesn't pay the grower to pick them up, and if he picked them up, there would be no one to buy them in the markets. There is an abundance of all kinds of food. The farmers have demonstrated this by giving away beef and there is no shortage nor need there be any shortage of clothing because the woollen mills are all closing down one after another, but the sheep are still growing wool, and the farmers are still shearing them but they can't sell it. So here we are with two of the basic needs, quite unnecessarily short in New Zealand. We also have an abundance of timber and we have lots of carpenters so that if you want shelter you don't have to go into a tent in the middle of winter. Even if you have to build a temporary shelter, you've got plenty of materials to do it. So this is now a socio-economic problem, not a charitable problem. And I resent the responsibility I've got of going to the Courts or going and pleading for people.

And that really started the popularity of my broadcasts because this was on a Man-in-the-Street session and these were the sentiments which were expressed in that way and were echoed by everybody who recognised the truth, except the politicians. The blame couldn't necessarily be placed at the door of such people as Adam Hamilton. He was a very, very conservative man and a very honest man and a very dull man, and he shared the lack of quality with most of his colleagues. They were completely and utterly frustrated. They didn't know how to handle it and all they could do was to try and block anyone who suggested something that might appear to be anti to the Minister of Unemployment's efforts to pay out 10/- a week for single, and 30/- a week for married men. The only reason they didn't stop me and cancel the licence was that I was a minister of religion and you were allowed in those days to broadcast on matters of religious concern. But you weren't allowed to broadcast on politics. George Bernard Shaw was refused the right to read a prologue to one of his plays because it was political. I thoroughly confused them because I was talking as a minister of religion and I was pretty well known as a broadcaster. So they were trying to find a way of how to ban me, without breaking this one right that you had. You could talk about devotional matters, you could conduct devotional sessions, you could broadcast church services until you were black in the face. But when you started to talk on what I'd said was Christian ethics, and I was a minister of religion, they just were flummoxed.

The Friendly Road happened because the broadcasting of religion was a permissable thing. So, all right, every station put on some devotional session because that was the only time anyone could say anything—in a devotional session. Then people who ran radio stations in those days would invite different churches. The churches didn't recognise the value of this or the potential of it, and so they would usually pass it over to supernumeraries. A supernumerary is one who is past his prime, and who has been retired. And in the church it means something quite different to a superannuitant. So they handed all these things over to these poor old gentlemen, nice and lovely fellows, but they'd got a bit creaky in the joints. And even worse, because they couldn't understand this microphone business, they were hopeless failures. So then they started to fail, they started not to turn up, there were excuses of sickness. And people like Lewis Eady's who ran 1ZR, which was the first station I started with, would immediately ring me and ask me to come down straight away because the Reverend so and so was supposed to take the devotional service and he's ill. So it was a few hundred yards' sprint and I'd get down there. I'd no idea what I was going to say. I looked along a shelf of books and I would see there "The Song of the Earth". That's all I had, just "The Song of the Earth", Nature's perpetual renewance—and just go on from there and talk for perhaps 12 minutes—and the

Relief depot, February 1932. Photo Alexander Turnbull Library.

Uncle Scrim's mission in Auckland had a fence before the riots. The palings were torn off to smash windows during the Auckland riots in 1932. "A fitting use for the property of the Methodist Church," said Scrim on radio the next day, much to the disgust of the church hierarchy. Photo C.G. Scrimgeour.

next day go along and do the same thing because the other minister hadn't turned up, until finally I found out I was going five days a week. Lewis Eady's, who operated the station, were very happy about it because they had a good audience, and I wasn't unhappy about it. There was no money required—I got no payment—but there was no money required and that was the way in which it started. The Friendly Road became this: I was talking first of all for the Presbyterians who were sick, I was talking for the Methodists who were too tired or were sick, I was talking for the other blokes who might have been Church of Christ or something else—but I knew that I was talking to people who would listen to a message, and that's how it became sort of a general thing that did not have any overtones of sectarianism.

The Man-in-the-Street session was quite a different matter.

The Man-in-the-Street radio programme had no particular religious overtones. The Man-in-the-Street was only protected because I happened to be the Rev C.G. Scrimgeour, not because I was delivering a message or religion. The Man-in-the-Street was a change of tone altogether, that is, I wasn't talking to sick people in hospitals. I wasn't pretending to. It's never been any mystery to me why it succeeded because it was humanising something that was a mechanical means of communication. And it was only this humanising effect, which was purely accidental, it was no clever divining on my part, it was simply accidental. I took that microphone and would not treat it as an extraneous thing—I took it as *the* thing, it was the person's ear—and I treated it rather, I think, quite scientifically, that is I never raised my voice. I spoke quietly. If I wanted emphasis I made the emphasis not in loudness as a tub-thumping preacher or as a politician would do, I made the emphasis in the same quiet tone and I always added the question "You tell me."

There were a lot of people who were afraid of this scrutiny I was putting them under. Do you know that in the early days that if the press wanted to destroy a politician, they just didn't publish his name. Next election he was out. But in the 1930s they were afraid of this new thing, radio. And if I said, say that a politician was being discarded and being disregarded by the press, or I said I met William Parry the other day, or I met Bill Jordan the other day, or I met someone else the other day, that overcame the press barrier. The government politicians and the newspapers couldn't stop this—especially if I said Bill Jordan. Don't you forget that the opposition didn't only come from the government. The opposition—the really fierce opposition to broadcasting—came from the press. There was no advertising then, so it wasn't because they were going to be robbed of revenue, but because of power. This was the thing that they really didn't like. If you wanted to kill a man in politics just don't mention his name. Their reaction had nothing to do with fear of advertising revenue, it was just simply fear of someone being able to contradict their power of destruction. And their power of destruction was pretty high. I had seventeen front pages of *Truth*, all attacking me bitterly because they thought they could destroy me by their power. But they didn't. They had a good go at it though, all kinds of tricks. And that I think was where radio was being born—it was coming out of its pre-birth state and it started to be shown up in its real power and its force and when you look at a programme like *Gallery* today or any public affairs programme, you see their enormous power.

Photo C.G. Scrimgeour.

STRICTLY NON—CONTROVERSIAL

No non-establishment views were allowed on radio although "Uncle Scrim" managed some new variations on biblical texts. But even he was jammed by government order in 1935 just before the election. The government bungled the job and the jamming contributed to the discredit of the government and the Labour landslide later the same month. Photo The Phoenix 1933.

Labour Comes To Power

Elections come, and elections go, and not all of them linger in the memory. I don't think any will be as memorable as the election of 1935, when Labour first swept into power. When the returns came in that night, I'm sure there were a lot of so-called "floating" voters who surprised themselves at what they had done. They not only turned out the political parties which had been governing New Zealand right from the inception of our parliamentary system, but they did it so overwhelmingly that it amounted almost to a revolution. And revolutionary it was when you consider that many of the leaders of the new government, now to be cabinet ministers, were thought of not so many years before as street corner agitators and "red feds", some of whom went to gaol rather than fight in the first world war.

I'm not sure of the exact figures now, but from memory Labour went into that election with about 24 members in the House and came out with 55. What a resounding victory it was, what a radical change in the direction of New Zealand's political mainstream! The government of the day was a coalition of the old Reform (or Conservative) and United (or Liberal) parties. When the great Depression hit the country in the early thirties, these two parties joined together to guide New Zealand through the hazards of those desperate times. They were led by a kindly farmer from North Canterbury, George Forbes, known to his friends as "Honest George". But honesty, admirable virtue though it is, wasn't enough. The government had no "go" in it. When the election loomed up in 1934, the government postponed it for a year, hoping that things would be better by 1935. If anything, the "stolen year", as it was called, made matters worse for them. People resented it, and the Labour promises of widespread social change made an irresistible appeal to the electorate. The stage was set, the fuse was lit, and on that fateful night in 1935, it all went off with a bang that was heard around the world.

All this is familiar to members of my generation, especially the agonies of the Depression. They were very real agonies on the North Canterbury farm of my girlfriend's family, where revenue was counted in shillings and pence, and humiliating sessions with bankers and mortgagors had to be endured at intervals if the farm was to be kept. By comparison I was a fortunate town boy who managed to hold on to his job right through, at a steady four pounds a week. Doesn't sound much today, does it, eight dollars for a qualified tradesman, but the cost of living was so low that even this small wage left something over for luxuries.

Everybody's Uncle—Mick Savage and friend. Photo C.G. Scrimgeour.

I had enough to spare, anyway, to buy my girl a "wireless set", as the radio was called in those days. It was a tall, black, handsome affair, with six valves, a Crosly Cabinet Console if you please. I installed it in the living room, put up an aerial, plugged in, tuned to 3YA, and we all settled back to enjoy this new-fangled marvel. It was such a novelty that the neighbours were invited for listening sessions.

Well, it so happened that all this was just before the 1935 elections. There was some excitement, I can tell you, when it was realised that we would be able to hear the results immediately they became available. In 1935 most homes had no radio, and in the country, election results were something you read about in the newspapers later on. The family decided to make a night of it. Invitations were sent out to friends and neighbours, extra cakes were baked, spare seats brought in, and sharp at 7.30 I tuned in and we all sat back to listen. I can tell you, I felt pretty important about it all.

But among these farmers and their wives I was suspect politically, and before the night was over, the wireless set was too. I was suspect because, well, I was a townie, but mainly because my father had stood against George Forbes in 1931, and this time my boss was doing the same thing. In the course of my work I had got to know the prime minister personally, and I had always found him to be a thorough gentleman, and indeed I had cast my first-ever vote for him that day. But as the first results came over the air, heavily in favour of Labour, some of the bloom rubbed off the novelty of the evening, and the Crosly Cabinet Console gradually became an alien thing, announcing news nobody particularly wanted to hear or believe, a gadget they could well do without after all—and some of this probably applied to the city slicker working the dials.

Of all those present who projected this growing feeling of hostility and disapproval, none was more notable than my girlfriend's Uncle Harry, a farmer from Southland, who was visiting at the time. He was a large gaunt man who smoked a big pipe incessantly, of the type we used to call a "chin-warmer". He was sitting there now, in the best armchair, hidden behind the morning paper, sending up clouds of tobacco smoke, saying not a word. He was a staunch conservative, and what he was thinking as the results came over the air, we could only guess. When he spoke, which wasn't often, he spoke with a rich Southland accent, with a burr as rough as matagouri. Where he came from, a talker was to be distrusted, and a smooth talker more so. At every fresh news that so-and-so had lost his seat to some Labour Party upstart, coming out of the black box in the cultured tones of Clive Drummond, then chief announcer at 3YA, there was a snort and another cloud of smoke went up from behind the newspaper, which was shaken and folded, and reshaken and refolded with such energy that the announcer's voice was all but drowned.

"Oh, my goodness!" said one of the women when the box announced that a cabinet minister had lost his seat. "Fancy that!" declared another as a conservative member of long standing fell by the wayside. "Begins to look like there might be a change of government," said a farmer neighbour, cautiously. And as I looked at the assembled faces, and watched their reactions to the results as they were announced, I began to suspect that not all these good country folk had voted for the Coalition that day, as I had imagined. In fact, now that Labour was beginning to look like a sure winner, there was a subtle difference to be noticed here and there. An odd remark about the need for a change, a suggestion of warmth when some Labour candidate unexpectedly won a seat, the occasional expression of furtive anticipation at some startling trend revealed by the figures. I sensed the gathering breaking into two political camps now that the chips were down, where I had thought there was only one.

"I'll get some supper," said my future mother-in-law, breaking the tension.

By the time she came back, the game was almost over. I remember she had a natty teapot thing with a little wick lamp underneath, which kept the tea warm if you happened to want another cup. She brought in a dinner wagon loaded with cream meringues and half a dozen other kinds of rich goodies—there mightn't be money about, but the cows were still in, and the hens still laying. In no time we were all chattering over tea and cakes, and the box in the corner, the Crosly Cabinet Console spelling out the most momentous news of the century, could scarcely be heard.

"Have a cup of tea, Harry," said my future mother-in-law, addressing her morning newspaper and the cloud of smoke. "Did you hear what the man just said, Labour's in."

The newspaper came down at last, and there was Uncle Harry. He took the pipe out of his mouth, and if his manners had not got the better of him, I think he would have knocked the proffered cup and saucer to the floor. He drew himself up to full height, a majestic figure of a man, wildly imposing, with grey beard, tousled hair, and blazing eyes. If the folded newspaper had been a tablet, he could have been Moses on Mount Ararat. The chatter fell away and a hush came over the gathering. Harry glared at each in turn, his eyes narrowed to slits. Oh yes, there were turncoats and traitors here, despicable people, politically anyway, who were capable of running with the hares and hunting with the hounds, people prepared to sell their votes for any old mess of cheap promises, weaklings not worthy of democracy's precious privileges. Beneath his piercing eyes they shuffled their feet now and looked at the floor. Harry wasted not one word on them. Then with magnificent dignity, with, as you might say, the royal flag of entrenched conservatism flying bravely, he strode from the room, smoke eddying in his wake.

And as he passed the Crosly Cabinet Console, I swear he spat at it.

I remember my father telling me, oh, lots of times about my mother and the 1935 election. They hadn't long been married I think, and the election came around, so my mother, who hadn't voted previously, went to her father and asked him how she ought to vote. He was a small businessman so of course he told her: "Vote for Forbes and Coates." Well my father asked her what her father had said and she told him. He almost had a fit. I still remember him telling the story: "Forbes and Coates!" he'd rage, and his face would get all red, even years afterwards when he was telling it. "Forbes and Coates! I told her if she didn't vote for Mick Savage she could leave my bloody house and never come back either." I don't know how she voted—she'd never say—but I suspect she put her mark beside the Labour candidate.

In those days if your family was well off you didn't hear much about the Labour Party except when father talked to mother about how terrible it would be if those people ever got into power. How we'd lose all our savings and what have you. In our family anyone who voted Labour, or even had a good word for them, was a rotter. I do remember that in 1935 there were pro-Labour slogans chalked on the footpaths. And it came as rather a shock to me to discover at school that I was the only one who wasn't a rotter.

I would say that that was the last time that I saw an election as genuinely a public event. I was in Cathedral Square in Christchurch on the night that the results were coming through. People didn't stay at home and listen to them from the radio in those days—they went out into the streets and saw them put up across the newspaper office buildings. And I can remember, there was nothing tumultuous about the reaction. People stood there quietly, but there was an undertone, a sort of growing sound as people responded to the election results as they came up. I think that they had been through too much. There was nothing comparable with the emotion, with the excitement,

Prime Minister Savage and his first Labour Cabinet pause briefly before proceeding to the socialist reconstruction of New Zealand. Photo Alexander Turnbull Library.

with the semi-hysteria of an armistice celebration, nothing like that at all. People didn't want to go singing into the streets or dancing or anything of that sort. There was a feeling everywhere of profound relief; it was as if they'd come to the end of a nightmare.

Of course in 1935 the Labour Party came into power. Can I remember it!—I'll never forget it. The only character in the whole district who had a job was the local power board chap whose job was something to do with the transmission lines that went past here, and he had a permanent job, a car and a radio. It was the only radio in the district, and it was considered a great privilege to be invited to his house say once a month to listen to the radio. I can remember putting on my good pants and us all going down to the Harris' place for the privilege of listening to the radio and thinking what a marvellous thing it was to be able to listen to a radio. This would be the only house in the district that had power in it too.

Well, everybody got invited on election night, and I can remember everybody there and the results started to come through. Every time there was a Labour victory—screams and cheers and people kissing each other, and whenever a Tory victory was announced—ugly growling and people's faces would change. Fairly early the urban results would come in—"Oh Jack Lee's in"—screams and shouts and stamping. Mick Savage got in, Peter Fraser and Paddy Webb and all these other characters. I think somebody must have produced a bottle, or two or three bottles and it was a memorable night. In a fairly close community like that people had got on each other's nerves in different ways over the grind of the previous two or three years, however long it was. But on this night everybody loved each other and everybody had a vision of a better future, they really did.

You used to go down to the relief depot, I think it was the Labour Department, and you'd stand there like it was a slave market, and they'd call your name. It would be just "Richards!" and you'd have to go forward and they'd treat you like dirt. It was no good complaining about it, they'd just show you the door and you wouldn't get the relief work. They had the power and they enjoyed using it.

But after Labour came to power it was a different story altogether. It was "*Mr* Richards" then, and there was no showing the door to anyone. The bloke that used to run the relief in Christchurch, the big man, the one in charge, after Labour came to power he wouldn't go home on his own after work for months afterwards. He was frightened half out of his wits. If the relief workers had got hold of him there wouldn't have been much left to try and put together afterwards. Labour's election really knocked the stuffing out of him.

It made a real difference when the Labour Party came in. We saw such a difference, for instance in the roads. All these broken down bridges and we were amazed at the bridges having no sides. Oh they were treacherous. If I happened to be driving I'd say to my husband "Oh, we're coming to one of those bridges. Change over." "Oh go on," he'd say, "you're a brave lady. Where's your faith?" "Oh," says I, "it'll take more'n a stretch of faith, it'll take a stretch of imagination to get over that bridge as far as I'm concerned. No. I'm not going to risk it." So of course when we used to go around the country after that, seeing the improvements, my husband used to say "Well, just look at these bridges. Just look at these roads. They're a memorial to Bob Semple." And they are. They still are. We mustn't forget the good work he did and also the rest of the Party. They really made a difference.

I remember one chappie saying to my husband when we came in—the elections were pending—he said "Who're you going to vote for Mr Hastie?" And he said "Oh, I don't know," (because we hadn't done any voting in New Zealand). "Oh," he said, "I don't know, one's as good as another." "Oh but they're not. You vote Labour and you'll have plenty of sugar." They called money sugar in those days. That tickled us of course. "You vote Labour," he says, "you'll have plenty of sugar." He said "You'll never have it with the National Party." And we used to hear that wherever we went. So of course they went in with flying colours. And from then on New Zealand seems to have gone apace because the Labour Party set the example to the National Party. They mended their ways you see, and then of course they vied with each other you see. What you can do, I can do better, you know, and so of course that was all good for the people.

There was great enthusiasm in 1935, everyone felt there'd be a difference. There was immense faith. The Labour Party then was composed of the old diehards whom we all knew. We knew Tim Armstrong, we knew Danny Sullivan, we knew Paddy Webb. We knew all these people, we knew their worth as much as we knew their weak points. But they were of us—of the working class we felt. Yes, there was immense enthusiasm, you began to notice an improvement almost immediately.

I think it must have been 1935 when my husband was working out at Rolleston doing this cutting and I think we got more pay for that. And then they organised the Parnassus work, PWD, and he went up there. And there he

ACCORDING TO PLAN

got four pounds a week and I got two pounds a week sent home to me, I was at home with the children on my own, and it was wonderful. I was able to buy a few little clothes, you know, it was wonderful having two pounds a week clear. We paid the rent and he just had to pay board for himself up there and after a while he and some others organised a community cookhouse and they could get their board much cheaper. It was a great thing up there, they had a cook and paid him in this co-operative thing—they bought in bulk and their board was much cheaper. That was the Labour Party that organised the PWD works which again was real work of course—they put that line through and that sort of thing. Yes, things were much better.

And business and trade began to pick up and when that work finished he got work at Sockburn out here with Alloy Steel at something like four pounds a week, or something like that. Wonderful. And we'd meet various people and they'd say their husband had a job at so and so and it was wonderful.

There were some people who didn't pick up, who'd always been depressed. This woman I knew had small children and her husband sold the shoes. I'd said to one of the women "Why doesn't she ask the parson for shoes because he's very kind, asking me if I wanted anything, and I know he'd give her shoes?" And she said that she'd had about four lots of shoes and her husband had sold them and that was that. Well, I didn't hear any more of this woman after the Depot was closed and after a time, round about 1935 I suppose—no Depots then—and this woman turned up. And she became cleaner of the school so I got to know her again, and all those children had a sort of hangdog outlook, you know, they were sort of . . . of course I suppose it was the environment a good deal and of course the Depression, but they never sort of recovered and came back as people in their own right. They always had this hangdog sort of look. I remember them going to school and being sort of outstandingly poor looking. I used to see a lot of the children of course being on the committee and living near.

Most people recovered from the Depression once they got in work again and were able to fend for themselves. There was a very sturdy independence amongst working people and it was the lack of that that got them down. I can remember myself the first time I went to the Depot and getting in the line for my turn and suddenly being overcome with emotion and going standing at the door looking at the Port Hills, crying. I thought how did it come that I should beg for bread. Then I thought well, who am I, these others are in the same boat, they're people just like me and I gradually got quite hard of course, but that was my first time. It does take something away from you, not being able to fend for yourself.

Aftermath

It's made an indelible mark on my thinking. Looking back and comparing what life was like then and what life is like now, it gives me a much greater appreciation of what people do when they're hungry and deprived. It also makes me think that commodities are just crap, that beyond a certain level, beyond certain human demands (which includes culture), a lot of things are completely unnecessary for my way of living, and I think it's given me a feeling of unity with working class people. I think I've got a genuine class-consciousness out of it which, whether it's rather illusory considering my relatively high income at this stage, still remains. I still identify myself with people who sell themselves and have no choice but to do so, and when they can't sell themselves then they—like in the Depression—they either break down or take to the grog or, as they did in 1935, vote for the Labour Party. I'm not sure which would have been the best thing to do in the long run.

Photo Alexander Turnbull Library.

Transcript typing by Nola Neas ★ Photo research by Caroline Martin, Jule Einhorn, Tony Simpson & Alister Taylor with the assistance of the Photographic Section of the Alexander Turnbull Library ★ Designed by Jule Einhorn ★ Photographic copying by Bill Beavis ★ Proofing assistance by Ian Fraser & Gil McGregor ★ Typeset by Armadillo Typesetting ★ Plates by Offset Plates Limited Wellington ★ Printed by Rotoset Limited Petone ★ Bound by Bookwork & Stationery Limited Palmerston North ★ Distributed by Quick Fox-ATP Martinborough ★ Edited and published by Alister Taylor.

Thanks for assistance with photographs to Dr W.B. Sutch, Max Riske, Jack Locke, NZ Herald, C.G. Scrimgeour, Jim Henderson, Auckland Public Library, Rotorua Museum, Lower Hutt Public Library, Evening Post, Connie Beardsley, Frank Renwick, Hocken Library, NZ Free Lance resources, Bill Mudgway, Auckland Weekly News sources, NZ Public Service Association Journal, General Assembly Library & others inadvertently not mentioned. Special thanks to the Alexander Turnbull Library and its Photographic Section staff & to Librarian Jim Traue & Deputy Librarian Ray Grover.

www.ingramcontent.com/pod-product-compliance
Lightning Source LLC
LaVergne TN
LVHW050646100826
845148LV00011B/2006